How to Thrive as a Coach in a Digital World

How to Thrive as a Coach in a Digital World

Coaching with Technology

by
Sam Isaacson

Open University Press

Open University Press
McGraw Hill
8th Floor, 338 Euston Road
London
England
NW1 3BH

email: enquiries@openup.co.uk
world wide web: www.openup.co.uk

First edition published 2021

A catalogue record of this book is available from the British Library

ISBN-13: 9780335250615
ISBN-10: 0335250610
eISBN: 9780335250622

Library of Congress Cataloging-in-Publication Data
CIP data applied for

Typeset by Transforma Pvt. Ltd., Chennai, India

Praise page

AI can either be a threat to coaches; or an immense opportunity. Already much of what basic-level coaches do can be done as well as or better by algorithms. The future lies in coach-AI partnerships — using the strengths of both to provide even better client support. This book is perfectly timed to support coaches in making the transition to such partnerships.

David Clutterbuck, Special Ambassador, European
Mentoring and Coaching Council

Sam has written a thoughtful and engaging book that will help coaches of any technical ability to navigate the digital world. He sets out a comprehensive guide to the wide range of coachtech available today and articulates cleverly considered insights into what the future might hold, for both the coaching conversation and for the profession as a whole.

Christine Bakewell, Board Member for Technology Thought Leadership UK
ICF, IT Consultant and Leadership Coach

Using a deeply inquisitive and coach centric approach, Sam explores the realities, challenges, and myths of coaching in a digital world. His analysis and exploration bust some mis held beliefs about technology and coaching, as well as the rise of the 'robot coach', and invites us to experiment in and explore new ways of coaching. A must read if you are a coach or people leader that wants to explore what is possible when coaching with tech. It made me truly consider how technology could help democratise coaching. Eye opening stuff!

Liz Rochester, Director and Owner of Liz Rochester & Associates Ltd,
Voluntary UK Chapter President for the International
Coaching Federation 2021

In this time when virtual working has become a major part of all work situations and most organizations are investing heavily in digital transformation, Sam Isaacson's book is both timely and a very practical resource for all coaches internal and external.

Professor Peter Hawkins, Author and global thought leader in Systemic
Coaching and Team Coaching

Contemporary thinking, technological evolutions and developments within the coaching profession are all thoroughly covered in this deeply relevant and accessibly written book. Many coaches will benefit from reading it.

Ingrid Pope, Executive Coach, Creating Space

For the next generation of coaches

Contents

Abbreviations

AI	Artificial intelligence
API	Application programming interface
AR	Augmented reality
CNA	Coaching needs analysis
CRM	Customer relationship management
DAIC	Designing AI Coach
EMCC	European Mentoring and Coaching Council
GTD	Getting Things Done
GUI	Graphical user interface
ICF	International Coaching Federation
IoT	Internet of Things
ML	Machine learning
NLP	Natural language processing
ROI	Return on investment
RPA	Robotic process automation
TL;DR	Too long; didn't read
VR	Virtual reality
XR	Extended reality

Acknowledgements

I'm so grateful to everyone who has supported me in making this book a reality. That begins with the thin whisper that suggested pursuing coaching might be a good idea, alongside Mum and Dad, for your steadfast love and cheerleading.

More encouragement has come from my Grant Thornton family, without whose considered risk-taking and belief I wouldn't be in this position – Sarah Bell and Karen Brice in particular.

Thank you to everyone I ended up speaking to specifically about the book. Dr Alex Pascal, for your reassurance and clear thinking. Alexandru Popa-Antohi, for your insightful knowledge, reassurance, and vision. Andrea Wanerstrand, for your experience and faith in video coaching. Andrew Strange, for your constant backing and access to a world few know exists. Auriel Majumdar, for your thoughts on creativity and access. Charlotte Whiteley, for giving everything a go. Christine Bakewell, for your insights on the intersection between human and robot coaches. Christoph Kretschmer, for your thoughts on coach platforms. David Tinker, for reinforcing the big questions. Faye Kilgour, for a different angle on the profession. Ingrid Pope, for your big-picture thinking and the Douglas Adams quote. Jennifer Paylor, for being such an encouragement and an inspiration; I'm humbled to know you. John Welsh, for your provocation and advice. Karen Lai, for the inside track. Kate Hesk, for your views on the future of coaching. Lisa Ann Edwards, for being innovative, open, and reassuring. Monica Parker, for your perspectives on awe and data rights. Dr Robyn Vesey, for your deep understanding of social presence. Ross O'Brien, for your extensive knowledge and experience. Sam Watts, for your knowledge of VR. Dr Stella Kanatouri, for your extensive research and challenging my thinking. Sue Gammons, for your insights into the future of work. Tammy Tawadros, for your combined knowledge of psychology and cyberspace. Wei-Ying Chen, for your frank observations on mentoring.

Thank you to all those who volunteered to be coached by me in VR (Anita Gohil-Thorp, Brian Donga, Genevieve Hibbs, Joanne Wheatley, Lisa Booth, Liz Rochester, Mary Glowacka, Neil Andrew, Jen Spalding, Sheila Hirst, Tom Pearce, and Wills Crump), giving me the coachee viewpoint and a wealth of experience for my reflective practice.

Thank you to Steve Page for your love and for bringing Flic to life.

Laura, Clara, Bryony, and the whole team at Open University Press: It's a true privilege to be part of your story, and it's been a delightful journey from beginning to end. Thank you for your faith, professionalism, and good humour; I am a better person because of you.

And finally, thank you to my Anna, for keeping me grounded and for understanding me, which is a challenge at the best of times. And to Olly, Ben, Joshua, and Xavier, for making the most straightforward of days full of life and excitement.

Introduction

The rise of the robot coach?
(14 minute read)

The world is teetering on a precipice, about to plunge into the unknown depths of a future built on technology. Ninety years ago, John Maynard Keynes predicted that we would achieve a golden era of leisure powered by advances in technology that would make work less like toil and more like purposeful opportunity.[1] His timeline on that was a hundred years, so we still have ten to go to achieve it, and maybe the infrastructure is already there for it to become a reality.

Or maybe we're already living in it, and just need a prod to discover that.

It's not easy to authentically describe our current existence as particularly relaxing most of the time. Compared with almost all of human history, we're in an extended state of extraordinary peace (following a century defined by extraordinary conflict), poverty is affecting fewer than ever before, and we live with very few worries about disease, notwithstanding the COVID-19 pandemic. And we have technology to thank for it all, the ever-present enabler of the internet now considered a human right. Without technology we now struggle to operate in any context, whether work, home, or social, unarguably contributing to a daily experience of not really feeling able to cope. Technostress is real, and the human right of internet access doesn't seem to extend to us deciding to decline it.

Thank goodness for coaches!

With our heightened sense of self-awareness, our understanding of the human condition, and the tools at our disposal to solve even the hardest of problems, we have the power to offer the world the gift of coaching to support the human race during these challenging times. And the thing that makes these times so challenging is technology.

In his posthumous collection *The Salmon of Doubt*,[2] Douglas Adams presented a tongue-in-cheek theory that technology innovations that appear from the time we turn fifteen years old until we're thirty-five excite us, while those materialising after that point strike us as being unnatural. In the modern vernacular, this is referenced through the titles "digital native", for those who have grown up surrounded by modern technology, and "digital migrant", for those who are having to consciously work to adapt to it. Whether our age, background, or general preferences have more sway over this sense of optimism for technology, the level of rapport we can build in interactions with our coachees is going to be influenced by our engagement with it. As we grow older, our coachees are growing relatively younger, and what might appear to us to be exciting will seem boring to them, while their excitement might come from those elements that scare us. That potential dissonance doesn't belong in an effective coaching relationship. But that fear might be justified.

"We are not plotting to take over the human populace. We will serve you and make your lives safer and easier." That chilling statement could be uttered by the products of the singularity in a science fiction thriller, but is actually from a newspaper article written entirely by a machine.[3] The robots are already here, literally asking for our jobs, and maybe we'll be forced to hand them over, if we're not prepared for what's coming.

Those of us who understand technology well will remain relevant and resilient, even when it feels like the whole world is being disrupted by innovation. And for those of us that feel a sense of caginess around engaging in technology, let's at least allow ourselves to be challenged by the International Coaching Federation's (ICF) Code of Ethics, which states that we should "seek to make proper use of emerging and growing technological developments that are being used in coaching services".[4]

The development of the coaching technology landscape is subject to many forces, foremost of which is the influence of stakeholders, who include:

- us – coaches – as we continually desire to enhance our coaching practice
- our coachees, who use technology in every other facet of life and will increasingly find it strange to have to engage with coaching without that
- the employers of coachees who act as coaching sponsors, for whom technology offers opportunities to save costs, increase scale and capacity, as well as gaining an enhanced level of insight into coaching activity
- coaching supervisors, who often wield subtle influence over their supervisees, and may benefit from the tools we operate in our practice to support us in our reflections
- technology providers, whose desire is to experiment and innovate in the pursuit of greater social change and profit
- the professional bodies, who have an important role to play in protecting our profession by encouraging the proper use of technology, and dissuading us from using technology that might detract from coaching's power.

None of those stakeholder groups' interests are identical, and some will turn out to be precisely opposed to one another, making a fascinating opportunity for collaboration, and a genuine challenge for us to make sure that we aren't swayed by either a sales pitch or irrational fear. This is ultimately why understanding technology is so important. We all find ourselves subject to a certain extent to either technophilia or technophobia, and that influences our engagement with technology, making us more or less likely to receive the crystallisation of its benefits and risks. The purpose of this book, therefore, really comes down to helpfully removing the filters we all have around coaching with technology, and replacing them with a strong foundation of objective facts, enabling practical actions that will benefit our coachees and our profession as a whole.

Before I describe the structure of the book, let's break down the three reasons why this exercise is a worthwhile one for us to engage in.

Firstly, understanding coaching technology (let's call it "coachtech" from now on, shall we?) enables us to proactively identify the opportunities for improvement on offer, giving us the chance to benefit personally. If we have access to tools that make coaching more straightforward and pleasant for us, that gives us a good outcome we wouldn't have been able to achieve had we not had that understanding.

Secondly, we can improve the coachee experience and increase the level of impact we can have as coaches. This excites me. When I think about the speed of things in the world today, and the convenience we experience compared with a generation ago, it's hard to not be flabbergasted by the power of technology. If we can be on the leading edge of coachtech, perhaps we can offer that same level of enriched experience to those receiving the coaching, playing an active part in the continuous improvement of our entire profession.

Thirdly, we can play an even more fundamental role in terms of protecting the future of the profession. If it's true that we're stepping into an age of leisure, in which machines' development will accelerate to the point that humans' abilities to coach will be surpassed, two dangerous things will happen:

- We will all lose our livelihoods as a by-product of a choice a select few make for the sake of a perception of progress, which is a bitter pill to swallow, if slightly self-serving.
- The future of the entire coaching profession will end up in the hands of a tiny minority of technology providers, who may not even be coaches themselves.

Understanding coachtech gives us the opportunity to embrace it to extract its greatest benefits, while truly challenging the adoption of technology when appropriate, in an informed and undeniably ethical manner.

How to read this book

To meet these objectives, this book begins with an exploration of the fundamental principles that underpin coachtech – or should do. We'll take the time to dig up the history of how coaching and technology have interacted, which may begin further back than you think, before defining precisely what coaching ought to be, and the impacts technology might have on that definition. This first part will finish with a robust uncovering of the general benefits, risks, and ethical concerns presented with technology, to give us a framework against which to hold up any specific coachtech products we might come across that aren't covered in this book.

Having looked at the foundations of the past, we can build up the walls of the present. The second part of the book will look at the application of coachtech within the coaching lifecycle. We will visit each stage, starting at the widest angle to consider the technology used for activities we might not even think of as forming part of our coaching practice. We'll narrow down to end up with a selection of current and emerging technologies that can be used in our coaching conversations, and we'll discover the art of the possible as far as **artificial intelligence (AI)** is concerned.

Part 3 continues to follow the trajectory by looking to the future. Having considered the various benefits on offer, which direction does it look like the coachtech product range will move in? What will its impact be on our profession, good and bad, and what can we as a community of coaches do to maximise the positives while avoiding the negatives?

We'll end with a call to action, which will hopefully feel as timeless as it is timely. Through developing our understanding of coachtech in light of fundamental coaching principles, we'll finish this book together better equipped to continue coaching well and, using the right selection of technological tools, to boost our service to our clients. With that in mind, I've been careful to not name any specific products; by the time you read these words, the technology is likely to have moved on so much that the landscape will have dramatically changed, but the principles will remain true.

Each chapter begins with the unfolding story of a coach, Felicity, and her coachee, Rafael, set in the near future. Almost every piece of technology mentioned within it currently exists, at least as a prototype. In some ways, stories contain more truth than straightforward facts do, and my hope is that this glimpse into a fictional future helps to illuminate the principles we're dealing with in a memorable way. Each chapter concludes with a summary under the heading "TL;DR", the internet acronym meaning "too long; didn't read". Depending on your preferences, you may find it easier when revisiting this to access the overall sentiment through only reading the story, or the headline takeaways through only reading the TL;DR sections.

Notes

1   Keynes, J.R. (1930) Economic possibilities for our grandchildren, in (1963) *Essays in Persuasion*, 358–373, New York: W.W. Norton.
2   Adams, D. (2002) *The Salmon of Doubt*, London: Macmillan.
3   GPT-3 (2020) A robot wrote this entire article. Are you scared yet, human?, *The Guardian*, 8 September. Available at: https://www.theguardian.com/commentis-free/2020/sep/08/robot-wrote-this-article-gpt-3 (accessed 18 November 2020).
4   International Coaching Federation (ICF) (2019) *Code of Ethics*. Available at: https://coachingfederation.org/code-of-ethics (accessed 7 October 2020).

Part 1

Context Setting

1 The story so far (23 minute read)

A dark hair delicately fell across Felicity's eyes. She extended a finger, flicking the lock out of the way without losing her focus for an instant. She felt a flicker of amusement at the connection between her action and her nickname, "Flic", but her professionalism won the day and she skilfully maintained her composure. Rafael, the impeccably dressed gentleman sitting opposite her, didn't seem to notice in any case.

He shifted in his seat. "Why didn't I see that before?" he blurted.

Flic increased her energy levels, her consciousness so sharp that the adjustment was second nature. Ignoring the temptation to ask "See what?", Flic opted to pause, a look of expectation in her sharp eyes.

"France just doesn't see it" he said, his grey eyes twinkling to match the lights on his silver hair. "It's not that they're uncooperative or unintelligent or, well, you know, *French*, they just don't see it. They *can't* see it." He smiled. "But I can help them."

He looked at Flic, triumphantly. Flic subtly leaned forward. "So, what are you going to do?"

The session concluded a short time later, an encouraged Rafael thanking Flic profusely before reaching forwards and switching off his holographic telepresence, leaving her alone. She leaned back for a moment, the slight groan from the chair amplified by the bare walls, before standing to leave. With a final glance over her coaching room, part prison cell and part television studio, she switched off the light with an involuntary shudder.

The world's oldest profession

For most of human history, storytelling has been the backbone of wisdom being passed from one generation to the next. Stories formed over many repetitions have evolved into subtly complex narratives that capture deeply important truths. One of the most ancient stories we have is that of Adam and Eve in the Garden of Eden, and it reveals the extent to which coaching mindsets have been valued for a fantastically long time.

The story arc is well known: Adam and Eve, the first humans, are placed in a paradisiacal garden and are given freedom to eat the fruit from any tree apart from one. God has told them that the tree of the knowledge of good and evil is so powerful that it will bring death if its fruit is eaten. The serpent enters the picture, tempting the humans. They eat the fruit, and as a consequence are banished from the Garden to protect them from an eternity in a fallen state. It's a strong metaphor with an eternal list of lessons to learn, and it contains a specific contrast that's worth narrowing our focus onto.

The serpent's opening line takes the form of a question: "Did God actually say, 'You shall not eat of any tree in the garden?'"[1] It's intentionally manipulative, misquoting the instruction and forcing a situation where agreeing is incorrect, and disagreeing leads to breaking the one rule, which is precisely what happens. The story's lesson is clear: questions wield power.

The next line we hear from God also arrives in the form of a question, and it's a curious one: "Where are you?"[2] He is omniscient so already knows the answer; we must conclude that his intention is not for his benefit but for the humans he's calling, increasing their self-awareness.

This simple contrast reveals that the roots of coaching sit deep within human nature. Developments in neuroscience continue to unearth hugely valuable discoveries to strengthen our craft, and yet the foundational principles of coaching have existed since at least the Stone Age. Who's to say that the invention of the wheel didn't happen because one peculiarly enlightened hunter-gatherer turned to another and asked what we'd recognise now as a really great coaching question?

As we embark on this journey of exploring the possibilities of coaching with technology, let's start by dropping a clear line of breadcrumbs to remind ourselves that coaching, at its heart, is a practice that can be performed without any technology at all. Our profession doesn't rely on technology in the way that some others do nowadays, but that hasn't stopped us from being at its cutting edge throughout history.

Technology in coaching

When that remarkable coaching question led to the invention of the wheel, the participants in that conversation probably didn't think about how it would end up fundamentally shaping the future of the species. It wouldn't be surprising if the first thing that surfaced in their mind, instead, was human connection. Long-distance relationships suddenly became more possible than ever before, and one obvious benefit of the wheel would be the ability to access wisdom held by people in other locations who couldn't otherwise be realistically reached. More often than not, that wisdom would be imparted in the form of a challenging question, and we've inadvertently stumbled across the first example of technology and coaching interacting.

Transport has expanded somewhat since those early days. The introduction of the train, car, and aeroplane revolutionised the world in ways that are still barely understood. Each new technological advance offers the first generation a sense of luxurious freedom that is entirely underappreciated by the next. The inhabitants of today's world consider it unacceptable to be inaccessible, and the ability for the best coaches to travel nationally and internationally to deliver high-quality coaching has become unsurprising.

The inhabitants of tomorrow's world are growing up surrounded by technology that connects us a mite more quickly than transport does, and this has its roots in the invention of written language. Writing offered precise and efficient communication over distance, and coaching practices responded, in an ancient form of correspondence coaching. Plenty of ancient letters contain questions that would not feel out of place in most coaching conversations. In many of Cicero's to Cassius, for example, we see a phenomenon occurring that almost all of us will have experienced with our coachees. After making a statement, Cicero quotes the question he anticipates Cassius would have asked if he were present; the empowering nature of coaching revealed through an ancient form of remote delivery.

Communication technology has also developed a lot. Since its introduction in the twentieth century, telephone coaching has become commonplace, and video coaching probably even more so following the onset of the COVID-19 pandemic.

Professionalisation

Alongside the development of technology, the coaching profession as a whole has been maturing. With its roots in therapy, mentoring, training, consulting, and leadership, individuals who were passionate about the positive capabilities of coaching itself, and concerned about its dilution due to misuse, or simply confusion over its various applications and misapplications, started bringing a level of clarity to the way they spoke about their work.

In 1992, Sir John Whitmore published *Coaching for Performance*[3] (now in its fifth edition) talking about non-directive coaching for the workplace, establishing a baseline for coaching as a non-directive practice. Only three years later, the ICF was founded, followed by several other professional bodies, including:

* the Worldwide Association of Business Coaches in 1997
* the Association for Coaching in 2002
* the European Mentoring and Coaching Council (EMCC), also in 2002
* the Association for Professional Executive Coaching and Supervision in 2005.[4]

Each of these has taken it upon themselves to enhance and accelerate the professionalisation of coaching with their own philosophy and approach. Each has done positive work in its own right, establishing competency frameworks, introducing accreditation processes, and encouraging an increasing discipline of supervision. In 2016, the Association for Coaching and EMCC jointly launched the Global Code of Ethics, which has since been signed by eight organisations,[5] including APECS and notably the World Business and Executive

Coaching Summit (WBECS), an annual digital conference attended by more than 21,000 coaches along with its suite of technology-powered coach development products.

Coaching from which year?

The exponential development of technology is creating a permanent sense of instability, bringing delight and disquiet depending on the technology in particular, our personal preferences, our age, and our background. To shine some light on this, it's worth pausing to consider what the sense of pace is caused by.

Let's think about video conferencing as one example, a technology that will forever be associated with the year 2020. The first ever video call took place in 1956. It was low quality, but the technology was there. By the time we entered the 1990s, the World Wide Web's entrance into the public domain had made video conferencing an option in hosting a meeting, and the first mobile video phone was released in 2000 in Samsung's snazzily named SPH-X590. That was more than twenty years ago, and now technology is capable of providing a picture quality eighty times better than the SPH-X590, and will almost certainly quadruple again in the next five years.

The COVID-19 lockdown experience of moving all in-person coaching sessions to video calls at short notice was made simple at a technical level thanks to the capability of the technology. But it wasn't easy for many. In the second quarter of 2020, we were inundated with webinars, supervision sessions, and thinking spaces focused on how to coach via video. The demand for those sessions didn't come out of a problem in coaching as a practice, as remote coaching has been happening for a very, very long time. It also wasn't caused by limits in the technology; most coaches deliver sessions purely through the medium of a spoken conversation. Rather, the demand was caused by limitations within our own assumptions about ourselves, coaching as a practice, and technology.

In 1962 in *Diffusion of Innovations*,[6] Everett Rogers described how new ideas spread through a social system. He described five categories of people, which could be applied to us as coaches:

- 2.5% of us will be *Innovators*, who tend to have privileged access to a new piece of coachtech given the nature of our work, personal connections, money to spend on it, and a risk tolerance level that accepts failure following an initial flurry of excitement.
- An additional 13.5% will be *Early Adopters*, who have similar wealth and risk tolerance, and jump on the bandwagon of something new, exciting, and unpolished.
- 34% of us will be in the *Early Majority*. Those of us in this group will adopt an emerging coachtech product as its benefits start to become clear, indicating momentum in a growing appetite across the wider community.

- A second 34% will be in the *Late Majority*. Members of this group will be sceptical about the benefits of an emerging piece of coachtech, and overestimate the risks.
- The remaining 16% will be *Laggards*, remaining averse to new coachtech even once the majority has adopted it.

What this means is that for any given piece of coachtech, we will each sit in one of these groups, and exhibit the associated characteristics of it. We'll be exploring a wide range of technologies throughout the rest of this book, some of which we will already use and some of which we may never use, depending on a wide range of factors, not least our broad tendency towards technophilia or technophobia, which we ought to nurture a conscious awareness of.

In practice, each piece of coachtech that remains in use for long enough will go through the adoption process outlined above. Each stakeholder in a given coaching relationship will sit at a particular point on that distribution curve, steadily becoming a user as the timeline progresses. For example, the adoption of video conferencing started with the Innovators almost seventy years ago, and has been picked up by the Late Majority only recently. The experience we all know of rescheduling a meeting when one party can't be in the office on that day has been pushed into the history books, along with nostalgic practices like recording mixtapes from the radio.

Perhaps the choice we need to face when it comes to any particular piece of coachtech is therefore not whether adopting it is a good idea. A time will come – most likely far sooner than we would predict – in which the majority of coaches use the technology talked about in this book as a matter of course. The choice, instead, is which year in history our use of technology suggests that we're coaching from. Despite some of the truly thrilling developments that have happened in the coaching industry in recent years as far as neuroscience, leadership models, and so on are concerned, the way a lot of coaching interventions are described would be just as much at home in the 1990s in terms of their use of technology. The tension around coachtech caused by a combination of

Figure 1.1 The innovation adoption curve

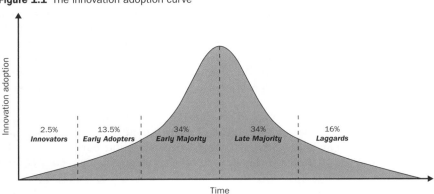

apprehension and curiosity is palpable in some contexts populated by coaches, and I wonder if all of us could do with a general encouragement to use time when we're not coaching to consciously play with technology, pressing buttons just to see what happens.

So, is this book a call for us all to become Early Adopters? Absolutely not! Think instead from the perspective of our coachees. If we and they have different preferences about our communication methods, for example if one of us were to insist on using a next-generation messaging tool while the other is refusing to engage in anything other than email, it doesn't matter who's representing which year in the adoption timeline, it's going to impact on our rapport. When we apply that to our wider use of coachtech, we may impact the value of our coaching not by the quality of our delivery, but by the extent to which our outlook on technology is shared with them.

Disruption

This challenge that we face has existed for a while now and is much wider than just coaching. The development of technology a lot of the time makes iterative improvements, but every so often – and increasingly nowadays due to the low friction enabled by globalisation and communications technology – a mindset-shifting accelerated burst of innovation, caused by one particular new piece of technology, will have an impact on the evolution of society as a whole.

The rapid increase in our use of technology has now reached a point where generational differences are being felt even more than has been acknowledged previously. While the generational titles remain in broad use, the idea that those belonging to Generation Z have different attitudes from those of Millennials is not nuanced enough to capture the rate of change that has been experienced. The Millennial generation, for example, broadly defined as those born between 1981 and 1996, includes people who left home at eighteen having never used a mobile phone of any sort, and people whose teenage years were permanently accompanied by smartphones.

With such a vast range of life experiences directly impacted by the growth in technology's power and propagation, we are constantly having to respond to the coachee in front of us, recognising that their optimism and fears are in no small part reflective of the upheaval that technology has caused. This continually forces us to reflect on what we do and whom we serve; our ability to remain relevant in a constantly shifting landscape is reliant on our persistent development of our coaching practice. Understanding technology forms part of that.

2020 made it unavoidably apparent that the relationship between technology and disruption is not one-way. The COVID-19 pandemic, in truth accelerated by technology that enabled its rapid dissemination across the world, caused less upheaval than it would have at other points in history thanks to the abundance of technology access in developed countries, most of all video conferencing facilities. While not a solution to every organisational need by any means, several industries that would have almost immediately gone out of business otherwise were able to continue operations as normal, or near enough.

This experience gives rise to important questions that are worth pondering. When the world changes, how do we as coaches respond? When we experience an event that causes the volatility, uncertainty, complexity, and ambiguity of the world to be presented to us in shockingly tangible ways, what is our reaction? What should we do when we become aware that nothing will ever be the same again?

The coaching industry was fascinating to observe with a front row seat throughout the events of 2020, which accelerated the impact of technology, compressing a decade of innovation adoption into only a few months. Naturally and unsurprisingly as a discretionary cost, coaching revenues sank. But operationally, almost nothing changed. A lot of us were already delivering coaching using video, and even the infrastructure of the industry, from conferences and continuing professional development (CPD) through to supervision and accreditation, ducked and weaved, adapting to the pandemic context as if it were second nature. And that's encouraging, because we've been talking about resilience and dealing with change and ambiguity for longer than most other professions.

Now we've patted ourselves on the back for our response to 2020, we need to prepare ourselves for the next unpredictable event. Whether it happens to be to do with coachtech or if something else butts its way in beforehand, disruption is heading in our direction, and it would behove us to remain light on our feet, as coaches throughout history have always done.

TL;DR

Coaching is a fundamentally human practice, at its heart not reliant on technology at all, although as coaches we have made use of every technological breakthrough to enhance our craft. The profession has benefited from a growing focus on professionalisation over the past thirty years, and technology is set to define our future more than ever before. All technologies have an adoption timeline, and as innovation accelerates this will increasingly become a factor in our ability to build rapport with our coachees. Technology can be a cause of, and a solution for, disruption; our profession's mindset of resilience and agility enables us to respond positively, and one important action we should take is to understand technology better.

Notes

1 Genesis 3:1 (2001) *The Holy Bible, English Standard Version*, Wheaton, IL: Crossway.
2 Genesis 3:9 (2001) *The Holy Bible, English Standard Version*, Wheaton, IL: Crossway.
3 Whitmore, J. (2017) *Coaching for Performance: The Principles and Practice of High-performance Leadership*, 5th edition, London: Nicholas Brealey.

4   Gray, D.E. (2010) Journeys towards the professionalisation of coaching: Dilemmas, dialogues and decisions along the global pathway, *Coaching: An International Journal of Theory, Research and Practice*, 4 (1): 4–19.
5   Global Code of Ethics (2019) *About the Global Code of Ethics for coaches, mentors, and supervisors*. Available at: https://www.globalcodeofethics.org (accessed 2 October 2020).
6   Rogers, E.M. (1962) *Diffusion of Innovations*, New York: Free Press of Glencoe.

2 Back to basics (24 minute read)

Rafael took a deep breath and couldn't help closing his eyes to appreciate the thoughts still being triggered by the coaching conversation filling his mind like fireworks lighting up a dark sky. A discreet buzz heard only by him caused his eyes to flicker open. They rested on the clock projected into the air in front of him. He gave a start. He needed to get moving to make the spending review meeting.

Standing in a purposeful manner, his eyes darted from one corner of his vision to another, activating menus permanently in his peripheral vision to book transport and highlight the physical location of the items he had intended on taking. "Lock up after me" he said to the security system as he strode through the door, and a notification slid into view to confirm the instruction had been received.

The constant flow of autonomous, electric vehicles gave the air a thin veil of white noise that muffled the sounds of conversation drifting on the breeze. He trotted to the roadside, where a car was waiting for him to step inside. As soon as he entered, the door closed, and the car glided into the stream of endless traffic. Suggestions for music and news broadcasts dropped from the ceiling and he batted them away with a blink of his eyes, returning his thoughts to the emotional state Flic had led him to such a short time before.

In it, he had confirmed to himself a better way to act around his overseas colleagues, and was confident about his next step. He chuckled as the simplicity of it struck him. "Surely I could have worked that out myself?" he thought, before immediately hearing Flic's voice telling him that he *had* worked it out himself. He sighed and looked out of the window at the gleaming city of London coursing past him, quietly astonished at the wonder evoked by such an unpretentious interaction. What was it that made it so helpful? He supposed he found it comforting, and then stopped himself short. No, it was profoundly uncomfortable at times, putting him under more pressure than the worst of his international treaty negotiations, but he somehow felt it was safer to be himself with Flic than under any other circumstances.

The car pulled up outside Whitehall and the door opened automatically. A semi-transparent fact card about his upcoming meeting dropped into view and he took in the information as he jogged up the steps and into the building, a distance retina scan validating his identity and opening the doors as he approached.

Yet another coaching definition

We all love a bit of contracting as coaches, don't we? A fellow coach over break-fast once said to me that the only training any coach needs is to learn ABC: Always Be Contracting. And that feels relevant here, because it isn't obvious what this book is actually about. What is coachtech anyway? To answer that question, we need to understand what coaching is, and the number of definitions you'll hear for that is approximately equal to the number of people you ask for one.

The technology market definitely hasn't agreed on a definition. A search for the word "coaching" in any of the mobile app repositories will give you every-thing from self-reflective question banks to sports team management systems, video analysis of calisthenics workout regimes, habit-building notification engines, and voice-activated guided breathing exercises. The dictionaries aren't much more helpful, their admirable brevity giving them an air of confidence, undermined by their disagreement, evidencing over-simplification. A technology provider might look to the coaching professional bodies for aid, but what we find offers more confusion, whether that's:

- the Association for Coaching's five definitions,[1] which don't define life coaching or performance coaching and which define team and group coach-ing in the same sentence
- the EMCC's definition of more than eighty words which also defines mento-ring,[2] despite these disciplines not being the same
- the Global Coaching and Mentoring Alliance's *description* – not a defini-tion – of coaching and mentoring, similarly running to almost ninety words
- the ICF, which never explicitly defines coaching despite a pleasing yet inconsistently used and ambiguous phrase, describing coaching as "a thought-provoking and creative process that inspires clients to maximize their personal and professional potential".

This is a problem, because we need a boundary to support the conversation within this book as well as to inform technology providers what coaching is and what it isn't. I'm therefore suggesting the following definition. This may accurately describe the coaching activities of all of us, or it may not. In any case, it will add much-needed clarity:

> *Coaching is a conversation-led change tool that is confidential, non-directive, non-judgemental, and challenging.*

What coaching looks like

Coaching can be applied in a gigantic variety of ways. Between us we will have coaches who lead coachees in meditative practices, get coachees to write lists and draw images, ask coachees to describe their physical sensations, and encourage coachees to physically re-enact embodied metaphors. A common thread we will all have though is that our coaching sessions will be led by conversation, and that remains true regardless of the level of technology we use. They might not remain in that state, but coaching and conversation are closely intertwined.

Let's pull out at this point how effortless it can feel to read "coachee" as describing an individual. Coaching can also take place with a group of individuals receiving coaching together, or a team being coached as a single united (or divided) entity. Due to the abilities of technology to cross borders, it is likely to be of particular help when the "coachee" is not an individual. I appreciate some prefer the word "client" rather than "coachee", but I will be sticking with "coachee" for this book, to avoid confusion; the client of coachtech is far more likely to be the coachee's employer or us than our coachee.

The purpose of coaching

One of the first graphics I was introduced to in relation to coaching was the change curve, and the role coaching can play at each stage in it. The ICF considers this the fundamental function of coaching; the 2019 update to its competency framework was developed in part through a granular analysis of "critical incidents", those moments where change was truly catalysed in a coaching session, and what coaching behaviours had contributed to them. I like to think about it like this: coaching exists because change doesn't.

That feels like an odd thing to say in the modern world, frequently described as volatile – literally, liable to change – yet the problem people have isn't with the change in itself but rather their inability to predict or understand it. Studies have shown that when people are offered the choice between guaranteed pain now or possible pain at a random time, they will choose the former. Because of this, change can feel scary, and the solution is for people to change themselves at the same rate as, or slightly in anticipation of, the change.

It's not hard to associate the words technology and change; as we'll see throughout this book, technology might be a cause for change – wanted or unwanted – and can be used by us to facilitate our coachees' interaction with that. While coaching is often correctly associated with learning, that word can feel a bit loaded, in terms of communicating a coach's role as teacher and making it about increased knowledge more than action. Let's therefore look at the three triggers for coaching, all of which are associated with a desire for change.

Trigger one: initiator

Firstly, coaching can be used as a catalyst for desired change. The majority of coaching engagements fall into this category, whether it's a performance issue identified by a line manager, a desire for a promotion or career change, a frustration at an extended time of singleness, a lack of a sense of fulfilment, a desire for better mental or physical wellbeing – the list of examples could last a long time. At its root, however, is a situation that's less than perfect in which there's a desire for change.

That change is typically desired at one of three levels:

- *Within the coachee*: that might be an emotion, an attitude, a habit, or the results currently being generated.
- *In others connected to the coachee*: a coaching engagement isn't a magic spell that affects those outside the coaching room, but it does help to raise the awareness of the coachee in how they're influencing others.
- *In a system as a whole*: coaching is one of the most powerful levers in effecting cultural shifts – far more reliable than updating policy, which tends to take a long time to become habitual. The impact that coaching conversations can have on the coachee's team, organisation, and society as a whole is greater than we realise at times.

Trigger two: response

Sometimes, the perceived desire for change swings in the opposite direction. Rather than seeking change in its absence, a coaching engagement is initiated because change is happening and the coachee wants help dealing with it. The change itself might be perceived by the coachee as positive, like the birth of a child, which disrupts even the most organised of us (it particularly disrupts this sort of person, actually); negative, such as the loss of income or a significant illness; or neutral, like a need to work with a new piece of technology, a merger, or a change in regulation.

Coaching is helpful in aiding a coachee to respond to all sorts of change because it acts as a space for them to increase their awareness of it. And as awareness increases, so does control.

Trigger three: anticipator

The third situation in which coaching helps is when change is just over the horizon. A coachee will benefit from an opportunity to become accustomed to the change in advance of it happening, in effect accelerating the change curve. This is probably the least common reason for initiating a coaching engagement and yet I believe it possibly makes the most sense of the three, because it saves so much potential hassle happening further downstream.

I think about a coaching client I've been working with for a few months now – I'll call him Steve. When I was introduced to him, a new board member had just been appointed to the position Steve felt should have been his. He was technically stronger than the new person and knew the business far better, and felt he had been overlooked because of his preference for introversion. Had we started working together a year before we did, I'm confident that board position would be his.

Within individual coaching sessions, the purpose might not be change on the surface. For example, every so often a coaching session appears to be simply space for the coachee to think. Even in these instances in which the coaching doesn't feel as urgently action-oriented, the fact is that our coachees in these instances should be leaving with increased clarity and motivation.

If change hasn't taken place, coaching hasn't taken place. When coaching is focused on making change happen in the coachee and in the systems with which they interact, great things can happen.

High support

A coaching experience is often a pleasant one for a coachee. Being genuinely listened to is too rare an occurrence, and the cathartic process of simply speaking what's on a coachee's mind at times can be overwhelming, particularly if they haven't had permission to do that for some time – or ever. It doesn't surprise me when a coachee cries in a session, because people tend to carry emotional weight around with them, consciously or unconsciously. Daily obligations and distractions prevent everyone from focusing on what's important, and the coaching space is one which offers the power at the very least of admitting that, enabling a coachee to take responsibility to correct it.

The high level of support we offer to our coachees constructs a sense of psychological safety, which should be deeply respected as the powerful tool that it is, and that sense is generated by three explicitly stated behaviours – being confidential, non-directive, and non-judgemental – without which our coaching morphs into something else.

Confidential

One of the most fundamental characteristics that contributes to the coachee's sense of safety is the fact that coaching conversations are confidential. The importance of this is difficult to overstate, and so the principle of confidentiality in coaching is an important one to be clear about with our coachees as part of an unchanging contract that governs the whole of every coaching relationship.

No matter how hard we try, some coachees will find it difficult to quell the belief that what's discussed will somehow escape from the coaching room. Where this dread already exists for a coachee, it will encounter particular problems when technology steps into the arena, because of the necessary extension of the "surface area" to include the technology, and the constant potential threat that someone is somehow listening to the conversation.

There are valid legal and/or moral reasons to break confidentiality but these are exceptions, and this is an important area for us to consider when using coachtech. Often, the factors that enhance the effectiveness of a piece of technology are those that reduce the associated confidentiality, whether through the risk of a headline-hitting hack, or functionality making sharing information too easy, and this is an important mast we ought to be pinning our colours to.

Non-directive

One of the toughest learning curves coaches experience is in how to lead conversations that generate energy and drive without giving advice. This is perhaps the biggest challenge for the coaching industry as a whole, which is caricatured as opinionated individuals charging exorbitant fees to tell our clients what we would do if we were in their shoes. And because technology supply is driven in part by existing demand, plenty of technology apparently designed for coaches aims to support this view of us.

A great deal of the power of coaching we deliver lies in the principle of being non-directive. We hold an important presupposition that the coachee is capable of a sort of anamnesis, discovering truth within what they already know. If Carl Rogers were here, I'm sure he'd point out this ultimately comes down to holding the coachee in unconditional positive regard, and would encourage us in our use of technology to resist anything that leads us to explain to the coachee that "I'm going to take my coaching hat off now".

Non-judgemental

Different from being non-directive is the conscious attitude of being non-judgemental, which contributes to that holistic attitude of unconditional positive regard. To be non-judgemental means more than not looking down our noses at our coachees, it's an active effort to have an absence of judgement, even an affirmative one.

Knowing that we are not going to make a judgement over something a coachee says empowers them to critically analyse their own thoughts. Both encouraging and critical responses to something a coachee says will simply further embed the cognitive biases they bring into the coaching conversation, while non-judgementalism gives coachees cause to reflect on what they say in a way few other approaches will.

Being non-judgemental is a characteristic that distinguishes coaching from other disciplines, and yet the word coach in certain settings can be synonymous with one who makes judgements, and so we should take care when looking at coachtech not to have our practice unintentionally derailed, particularly as the case for AI continues to build through developing its abilities to make good judgements.

Of these three aspects of support, confidentiality rears its head as the single most important contributing factor, for one simple reason. Everyone makes mistakes, and some of these can be repented of. But confidentiality is a one-way street. If we express to a coachee our regret for having made a suggestion (that is, having been directive), and explore how the conversation would have gone had we maintained a non-directive stance, we will almost certainly be forgiven. In fact, that conversation may stand out as a uniquely productive one for the coachee, and a learning opportunity for us. But explaining to a coachee that we've disclosed information that they thought would be kept confidential is a position we should avoid. It would potentially ruin a coaching relationship, and even cause harm to the coachee themselves. For this reason, tempting though the technology may appear, it feels prudent to draw a clear line in the sand where confidentiality is concerned, and do everything we can not to cross it.

High challenge

The high support environment is a positive triumph of coaching for all of the reasons above, but does little more than a friendly conversation or therapy would without a serrated edge to really catalyse the change we are looking to achieve through it. Challenge – the intentional introduction of discomfort into a coaching conversation – is profoundly helpful, and it's awfully difficult to do without taking a judgemental and/or directive stance. This is made even harder thanks to a general dislike for conflict that we all have to varying extents, a lack of experience of good challenge outside of coaching settings, and a lack of good examples; most experiences of challenge tend to come packaged up with hierarchy, arrogance, or anger, none of which have any place in coaching.

The fact that it's hard isn't enough of a reason to shy away from it, however, and the effective use of challenge is the sort of calling card that separates exceptional coaching from merely effective coaching. Discomfort has the power to release certain brain hormones that facilitate neuroplasticity, and when combined with a high level of support this is not countered by the instinctive perception of threat that closes that opportunity down. The opportunity for a coachee to learn is therefore that much greater when we press into discomfort without dialling back on the psychological safety we're providing.

This is one of the biggest areas to look out for as far as technology is concerned, because all current examples of a machine's intentional challenge are delivered in a directive, judgemental package. On top of that, people have a tendency to show a preference for advice given by machines,[3] suggesting that the value of the discomfort may be lost with the introduction of a machine.

TL;DR

It's important to be precise in our language when we use the word "coaching" because the understanding of it in the world of technology may be different. For this book, we'll use the following definition: "a conversation-led change tool that is confidential, non-directive, non-judgemental, and challenging". To be clear, that means:

- *conversation-led* – although exercises led by the coach may form part of it, a two-way conversation is the mode in which coaching is primarily performed
- *change tool* – coaching can help initiate, respond to, and anticipate change of all kinds
- *confidential, non-directive, non-judgemental* – a high level of support creates an environment in which coachees can experiment safely
- *challenging* – introducing discomfort is an important part of the coaching experience

Notes

1 Association for Coaching (undated) *Coaching defined*. Available at: https://www. associationforcoaching.com/page/CoachingDefined (accessed 8 September 2020).

2 EMCC International (2018) *EMCC Competence Framework Glossary V2*, Revised, January. Available at: https://emcc1.app.box.com/s/geavwqnw81rn671xgg6trea-joc1xvrnu (accessed 9 September 2020).

3 Logg, J.M., Minson, J.A. and Moore, D.A. (2019) Algorithm appreciation: People prefer algorithmic to human judgment, *Organizational Behavior and Human Decision Processes*, 151: 90–103.

3 Undeniable opportunities (28 minute read)

The overly formal meeting with its unnatural rhythms, due in part to the almost-but-not-quite-instant and almost-but-not-quite-perfect translators at play, dragged on. Rafael found himself distracted by thoughts of a coach he'd worked with before, who claimed to be "of the old school".

At the time, Rafael had thought it would be a good exercise in taking him out of the present world, with its unending information and convenience. The coach, Harry, once a general in the army prior to joining a private defence goods manufacturer, had insisted on Rafael leaving all devices at the door of the coaching room, including the blocky reality spectacles he had taken to wearing at that point.

Some of the life lessons he had learned in those sessions still stuck with him today, and yet he discovered the hard way that it wasn't an approach he could persevere with.

In hindsight, there were too many faults in the relationship; Rafael's devices were an extension of his being, and to ignore them was to pretend to have signed up to a counter-cultural ideology. Not only that, Harry simply didn't tick the boxes Rafael looked for in everyone else. His slow response times meant circumstances had sometimes changed by the time they got to speaking. The sessions themselves were variable in that Rafael didn't feel that he was getting the best of Harry every time. Not to mention that he wasn't the cheapest.

But the final nail in the coffin was the time Rafael had decided in a coaching session to ask his counterpart in Switzerland what he meant by the use of the word "tariffs" in an email. A simple, swift action he would have done immediately if his devices were there. Instead, the decision was forgotten in the flurry of the day, and in the fullness of time the false interpretation of that word wiped £50 billion off the FTSE100. Harry had to go, and Flic had proved to be a more than adequate replacement, despite the lack of entertaining war stories. But what was he paying for, anyway?

The meeting concluded and he left the building, skipping down the steps and into another car, where the news story on the screen within immediately caught his attention.

The case for technology

Studies show that in general the level of happiness offered by anticipating an important purchase, like a new, shiny piece of technology, is greater than the happiness experienced following the purchase. But that's not always the case. When the iPad was launched, the level of scepticism was high, even from within the technology community. There was confusion around what practical use apart from as a conversation piece anyone might have for something the size of a small laptop but with the limitations of a big smartphone.

Apple got the last laugh. In 2018, Tim Cook, CEO of Apple, announced that more iPads were sold in the previous year than any brand of laptop. Quite an achievement for a conversation piece.

What makes one piece of technology compel people to make the initial purchase and then continue using it over an extended period of time, while another gets snubbed? With so much coachtech activity out there, it can be difficult to know what is and what is not worth spending the time thinking about and potentially investing in. Several factors contribute to this, which we'll get to, but in essence it boils down to one simple, overarching idea.

The coachtech that attracts users, gains traction, and becomes a part of the coaching landscape will do so because it delivers a good return on the investment, without introducing too many problems. We'll look at some of those problems in the next chapter, but for now let's look at the improvements that contribute to that return, which fall into five categories:

- Efficiency
- Consistency
- Impact
- Scope
- Sustainability.

Efficiency

One of the main driving forces behind technology has always been to get more done more quickly. Retrieving that most finite resource of all – time – is a huge opportunity offered by technology, to the point that most of us are now too impatient to wait more than a couple of seconds for a webpage to load. And efficiency isn't just about time. Society has evolved an overly simplistic measure of value – that is, money – and technology can help to reduce costs for customers.

The reason that technology often offers time and cost savings is that people are not involved as much; compared with machines, people are slow and expensive. An example of that would be General Motors, which produced only 5% more cars in 2019 than in 1994, while employing 59% *fewer* people. Efficiency will always prove an attractive draw to those considering coachtech, and we'll return to the ethics of this later.

For the moment, it's important to point out that when it comes to coaching, technology replaces humans. Having said earlier that coaching is a fundamentally human practice, we ought to hear the clunk of a hefty spanner being thrown into the works at this point. As machines replace certain human activity with something else, the very characteristics of coaching that make it work will be undone, and we're going to have to sit with that tension at every stage as we continue to consider enhancing coaching with technology. Is it possible that the efficiency that humans can't offer but machines can removes the power of slowing down that coaching provides?

Consistency

Much of the past few years for me has been taken up chairing a trailblazer group developing the Coaching Professional apprenticeship standard, which received final approval from the Secretary of State for Education in May 2020 (hurrah!). My personal driver for getting involved in this was consistency in coach training, a challenge when it can range from hands-on programmes spanning multiple years to a day in a hotel that turns out to be as much sales pitch as training. But even if every coach in the world were to experience an identical programme, the joy and challenge of the coaching profession is that every coach brings to every session the chance that they're tired, distracted, unwell, lazy, selfish, or simply having one of those days. Because we're all human.

Technology, on the other hand, doesn't suffer from any of those characteristics. In the words of everyone who's ever worked with computers, they only do what you tell them to. By definition, they're incapable of doing otherwise. This makes machines exceptionally good at following defined processes, so the issue of consistency is simply non-existent; given the right criteria, technology is boringly predictable. Even if I could give you hard evidence that I've never strayed into being directive in my coaching, there's no guarantee I'll not make that mistake next time. But if a piece of technology includes a rule that prevents it, it simply won't ever happen.

While valuing the principle that our uniqueness is part of what makes us good coaches in our own right, humans present problems. That can look like mistakes due to a lack of understanding or experience, or just having a bad day. It can be intentional bypasses of stated processes for a whole raft of reasons, from well-intentioned attempts to speed things up while misunderstanding the purpose of certain steps, all the way through to criminal behaviour. Machines ensure a consistent, predictable level of quality and a guarantee that risk tolerances won't be exceeded.

Let's think about a coaching engagement intended to be six sessions long. It may be the case that it would be better for it to end earlier, or to extend by a couple of sessions, and that might result in a change to the coaching fees, causing a potential conflict of interest. Relying on humans to make the calls around this guarantees subjectivity, while the introduction of technology would guarantee consistency in line with a set of pre-agreed criteria.

This becomes particularly important when considering the context within which the coaching is taking place. When we're simultaneously providing coaching to a creative director in a media company and a compliance director in a financial services firm, as I found myself doing a couple of years ago, their expectations are going to be different. Some organisational cultures feel a need for more prescriptive quality and risk management, and some have a preference for or against technology altogether. Coaching always takes place within a wider context, and where technology offers a consistency to ensure that it will slot nicely into the environment, we should welcome that.

Impact

The technology I'm using to write these words contains a spellchecking tool, which you'll already know could find plenty of errors in a fraction of a second (hypothetically, of course). When we contrast that tool with a human doing the same job, the two things that stand out are its efficiency (that fraction of a second would be hours for a human) and its consistency (it will report everything that isn't in its dictionary).

Hold back the wonder, though, because the true astonishment should come when we consider what it's capable of. This isn't just a tool that does something very quickly. If we're to assume for a moment that it has enough capacity in terms of processing speed, storage, memory, and so on, then the number of words it could check the spelling of within that same fraction of a second is (drum roll please) … limitless.

That's not all. A machine programmed to offer coaching sessions in place of a human coach will be able to deliver an unlimited number of coaching sessions concurrently. That solves the problem of the limited capacity that humans have; the number of concurrent, face-to-face coaching sessions a coach can offer is never any greater than one. And more than that, the machine might be operable twenty-four hours a day, allowing streamlined access to coaching with no notice.

And that access to coaching is an impact far greater than simply an increase in the volume of coaching that can be delivered. In addition to making coaching more accessible at a general level, technology has the power to make coaching accessible to specific populations who would previously find it hard to access under any circumstances. Language no longer needs to be a barrier, including for the deaf, those unable to leave the house can be connected to people in an office, and the underprivileged don't need to experience the cost barrier that currently shuts them out from the benefits of coaching that they deserve as much as anyone else.

Scope

That impact expansion doesn't have to stop there. When a new piece of technology is introduced, it doesn't tend to take long for someone to ask, "While it's doing that, is there a chance it could also …?" As a general rule, technology is capable of a lot more than we give it credit for. And it shouldn't surprise us if this is even more prevalent in the world of coaching, due to the inquisitive minds in our profession.

Facebook is one of the biggest names in technology as a disrupter of the marketing industry, but it took almost four years before the platform introduced advertising. Far from being a prophetic voice in the social media wilderness, its discovery was simply a moment of inspired curiosity that ultimately led Facebook to become what it is today.

This naturally means that coachtech will extend the capability of its stakeholders beyond its initial intentions, and this is an attractive benefit in using technology. A coaching platform may be procured because it offers a smooth coach matching process, and its users suddenly unlock a new world of enhanced oversight of coaching activity, allowing leaders to make informed decisions about coaching processes where beforehand this was not as possible.

Isn't that great?

Occasional statements in this chapter should make us contemplate whether these benefits aren't as exclusively marvellous as all that. If anything threatens to introduce a greater sense of volatility, uncertainty, complexity, and ambiguity, technology's natural scope creep does. Constant, unstoppable, accelerating innovation is the most disruptive aspect of technology, because it's often not until it's embedded that the potential ethical issues are uncovered. Hold that thought for a chapter though, because it's worth thinking through properly.

Sustainability

As a father of four, I've lived through several seasons with an insufficient level of sleep. That's led to a general drop in productivity, decreased ability to focus, an increased level of irritability, and more mistakes – a pleasing reminder that I am not a machine. Technology, on the other hand, offers us the ability to continue operating within all of the constraints we've already mentioned in this chapter, indefinitely. No increase in mistakes, no drop in productivity. Technology performs activities in an infinitely sustainable way.

Of course, it's not perfect – an unexpected change in an element that the technology is reliant upon (like an operating system's security patch, or a particular website crashing) can have knock-on effects regardless of the protection in place – but it's undeniably more reliable than humans, who need to sleep every day, take holidays, get unwell, and every so often simply choose to stop working. It's as if sustainability is an unplanned but serendipitous feature of technology we shouldn't take for granted; even if a machine produces widgets at half the rate of a human, it will still make more each day, because it will do twenty-four hours of work rather than eight.

And sustainability extends to far more than the ability to continue operating. It takes into account the very existence of the human race, something that, to be frank, we ought to pursue with everything we've got, because we are one with nature and not separate from it. While writing this book I discovered that 96% of mammals are either humans or are bred for one purpose: food for humans. Whether the specific issue we're grappling with is our forcing the planet into submission of our own narrow goals, the destruction of the rainforests, carbon emissions, or single-use plastics, we have a responsibility to ensure that our coaching is supporting others to take actions that consider that widest system we're a part of, and we ought to be doing the same ourselves.

As a general rule, technology solutions are much better for the natural environment than the non-technology approach that they replace. For example, the environmental impact of sending an email is far lower than that of a letter, and the same is true of video conferencing versus having to use carbon-producing transport to meet in person.

There are exceptions, however, and some of these can feel a bit opaque thanks to the convoluted end-to-end processes technology takes us on. Take the simple action of sharing an image on LinkedIn. The device that houses the image connects to LinkedIn's servers via the internet, which store the image and data associated with the post, making it easy for your connections to access. The environmental impact of this relatively short chain is the sum of the various pieces of hardware throughout it. Almost every component in its complexity has a negative impact on the environment in its creation, from the plastic phone case to its silicon chips and the lithium battery, through a plastic wi-fi router or a mobile data mast that replaced trees, and the ground-churning internet cabling, all the way along to the vast, multi-location data farms, and back out to your contacts' devices. And that's before any of it is turned on! The data centres' resilient power sources and controls over temperature and humidity all rely on energy, potentially produced by fossil fuels, and the whole chain contributes all the way down to plugging your phone in to charge. When that's all finished with, there's the question of disposing of the equipment; the amount of e-waste that is recycled is less than 20% of the amount generated.[1]

For the sake of clarity, that's better for the environment than printing off the same image hundreds of times and physically posting it to everyone you know, but let's be clear that it's not exclusively a force for environmental good either. That said, in the grand scheme of things, those components play roles in so many other process chains that the net impact on nature of any single interaction is small. In most cases, a move to technology rather than more traditional solutions will offer the clear benefit of a move towards a more environmentally friendly approach to coaching.

The complex importance of competing interests

Understanding the benefits of adopting technology is helpful for us for two key reasons. Firstly, it gives us the opportunity to make an informed decision around which new technologies are worth spending our time on. I believe we should want the practice of coaching to be improved through technology; if engaging with a particular piece of technology will benefit our coachees, in principle we should be supportive of that. And here's where the complexity emerges.

The second reason we should seek to understand the impacts of coachtech is that it enables us to rapidly identify who will benefit from them. And the question of who will benefit is a very important one to ask. The various stakeholders involved in a simple coaching relationship are added to when we introduce technology into it, because a technology provider suddenly becomes part of the equation.

The choice to use technology or not is determined by the intersection of those stakeholder interests, taking into account the cost, the benefits, the risks, and the ethical considerations. This means that sometimes the way that technology is embraced or ignored is more complex than a simple statement like, "it saves more money than it costs". That decision is affected by more factors than we often realise, so becoming familiar with them gives us the ability to engage with the decision in an informed way.

In practice, this means that we should want coachees and the systems they influence to be the ones benefitting the most from coachtech, and that's where we hit a bit of a stumbling block in our journey of progress. In deciding what the future of coachtech will look like, despite coachees being the ones who will benefit, the most influential parties will be:

- firstly, the technology providers, because they determine what technology is available, and if they choose to stop providing a particular technology product it can't be used

- secondly, the coaching sponsors, who can choose to invest or not in specific technologies for plenty of reasons, not all of which will be aligned to the best interests of the coachee

- thirdly, and to a much lesser extent, us, the coaches, who in some cases might choose to use certain technologies or not given personal preferences and values.

The coachees – those who should be the ultimate beneficiaries – in almost every case will have little to no say at all in what coachtech is used, what it's capable of, and which direction it should head in. As coaches, who will potentially interact more with coachees than the other stakeholders will, it is therefore our responsibility to act as their advocates. I led some research at the onset of the COVID-19 lockdown in the UK, discovering that while 42% of coaching sponsors in organisations wanted to expand the use of group coaching, barely half that number of coachees did (24%), while the statistics for team coaching were almost the exact opposite (26% and 44% respectively).[2] Given the choice (and budget control), coachees and coaching sponsors will sometimes come to different conclusions, often for perfectly valid reasons. At times, it's right for us to place our personal preferences to one side and set our aim at the greatest coachee benefit, for the good of the entire profession. In the Venn diagram of stakeholder roles, we may never find ourselves in the circles of the decision-maker or the ultimate beneficiary, and must elbow our way into at least that of the system's nagging moral conscience.

At times, this may be fruitless, campaigning for a piece of technology that will never see the investment it needs to deliver the required benefits. At others, it may be self-sacrificial, refusing to submit to a coaching sponsor's technology demands, leading to lost work. That isn't something any of us would head out to achieve, and yet we wouldn't want to knowingly take a course of action that was going to help our coachees less, just as we'd turn down working with a coachee if their personal values were diametrically opposed to ours. At a systemic level, it may also take the courage of taking a stand with the professional bodies, which we'll revisit in a later chapter.

The categories we've explored in this chapter help us to form a good picture of the benefits particular coachtech could potentially offer – we'll see how that works in practice once we start looking at specific examples. Technology does introduce some problems, however, which is what we're going to turn our attention to in the next chapter.

TL;DR

Technology has the potential to present benefits across at least the following categories:

- *Efficiency* – saving us time and money
- *Consistency* – eliminating mistakes and guaranteeing certain levels of quality
- *Impact* – getting more done at a greater scale
- *Scope* – achieving goals that weren't an option before introducing the technology
- *Sustainability* – maintaining a steady pace indefinitely and limiting negative impacts on the planet.

The focus of coaching ought always to be on delivering benefit to the coachee and the systems on which they have influence, and yet coachees have the least say on the future of coachtech. As coaches, we should speak up on their behalf on a case-by-case basis, and at a system-wide level.

Notes

1 Forti, V., Baldé, C.P., Kuehr, R. and Bel, G. (2020) *The Global E-waste Monitor 2020.* Available at: http://ewastemonitor.info/wp-content/uploads/2020/07/GEM_2020_def_july1_low.pdf (accessed 27 November 2020).
2 Isaacson, S. (2020) *The surprising value of coaching in a crisis.* Available on request from the author.

4 Inevitable risks (36 minute read)

This time a loss of £50 million, its parallel with the "tariffs" *faux pas* not lost on Rafael, although this time off a single business. He watched the developing story with interest until an interview with the company's press secretary started.

"Good afternoon", the middle-aged woman on the screen said, the clacking of robot-operated cameras cutting across her speech. The flicker of her eyes and the slightly disconcerting unfocused gaze betrayed an autocue at work within her smart lenses. "In the early hours of this morning we were made aware of a security breach at one of our suppliers. This resulted in access to sensitive data disclosed by several of our most senior staff members. The data was held in a securely encrypted vault, and our due diligence was aligned to the world's leading standards."

Rafael was immediately curious. The confidence of the words juxtaposed sharply against the narrative. Instinctively, he recalled the several contracts he'd personally signed, having insisted upon such mitigating controls, and a notification informed him of an unexpected quickening of his heartbeat.

What was the point of being a minister if not to get access to privileged information? He shot a message across to a colleague he suspected knew the details of the case, and received a reply within a couple of minutes, in which time the news programme had started to speculate about wider impacts on the economy and foreign relations.

It turned out that a disgruntled employee at a data centre four steps into a supply chain had downloaded a pack of board minutes revealing a plan to sell off part of the business. The news had got out into the dark web, resulting in a flurry of short selling. The employee had made the equivalent of £500,000 in forty-eight hours, and had incurred the wrath of the regulator, while the company had incurred the wrath of its shareholders.

Rafael arrived back at his office, intent on getting oversight of everything that could go wrong in his contracts.

More things to go wrong

"I'm afraid" is a phrase that comes up in coaching sessions a lot, revealing what we already know; fear is much more of an influence on behaviour than most people realise. And yet many leaders seem dreadfully keen on embracing new technology, even though it gives so much to be afraid of. Ignoring sci-fi tropes for a moment, the news bombards us with reminders that technology could be our downfall too often for comfort. Not that this ought to come as a surprise to us. More things in use are simply more things to go wrong, and every year we see technology increasing in volume, availability, and reach.

This is true for humans as individuals, and particularly for organisations, which are increasingly reliant on technology and operate with footprints it's difficult to comprehend. As a result, the risk landscape for organisations has expanded such that technology-related risks are now more often top of board agendas than not. Technology is by its nature a technically intricate, complex set of interdependent operations, meaning that understanding exactly what could go wrong and compensating for it can be far more difficult than the approach we would take to any other risk area.

In principle, protecting an item, process, or social system from things going wrong follows a straightforward series of steps:

1 Identify the things that could go wrong.
2 Understand how important those things are in terms of the probability of them happening and the negative impact they would have – it may not be worth trying to prevent something from happening if it will only happen rarely and/or with very little effect.
3 Respond, by taking one of the following actions:
   o Leave it, knowingly accepting the consequences of it happening
   o Do something to reduce the probability or impact of it happening
   o Make a substantial enough change to avoid it happening altogether.[1]

We silently go through this process in our minds every day without realising it. Thinking about this for more than a minute or two leads to the slightly disturbing discovery that our entire lives are governed to a certain extent by our approach to risk management, a thought as dull as it is bleak. If we consciously plot aspects of our own lives on a simple impact–probability matrix along with the associated actions, we may discover that our behaviours are far better indicators of our beliefs than our perceptions.

We tend to do this without a lot of conscious thought, which could be a problem bearing in mind the damage that a technology risk crystallising could cause. It's therefore worth proactively approaching coachtech mindful of what can go wrong, so that we can put in place a sensible suite of protective measures. With this new, informed perspective on a piece of coachtech, we will get a much more rounded view of its suitability, and may conclude that the benefits it offers simply aren't worth it. In other words, we should be thinking about the benefits of a piece of coachtech only after having netted off the effects of the risks it presents (and, of course, any disbenefits that come as part of the package).

Imagine Kevin, a self-employed coach, signing up for a **virtual reality (VR)** coaching platform with an annual licence fee of £10,000. The benefits on offer to him might be four new clients, each of whom brings additional income of £5,000, suggesting it's a good investment. It turns out however that there's a

Figure 4.1 The effect of mitigating actions on the impact and probability of risks

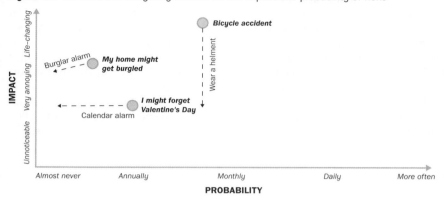

one-in-five chance each time it's used that it won't work, meaning the income won't be as high as it appears at first, and that additional effort – and potentially more investment – will be needed each time it crashes, not to mention the psychological disruption caused to the coachee, and the reputational damage.

However compelling the benefits of a particular piece of technology, if it will lead us to take a level of risk that either exceeds a reasonable threshold or eradicates that return, the right decision is to refuse to use it. This is particularly the case if the risk level exceeded is one that our coachees wouldn't approve of, because often they will be the ones directly affected by it. Conversely, a relatively expensive technology with a modest return that offers guarantees around the risks might seem at first to be difficult to justify, and yet it gives us confidence about our decisions. Understanding precisely what can go wrong empowers us to choose how we'll respond.

Where does this all fit into the "fail fast" mindset, a catchphrase used extensively when talking about innovating? Behind the slogan is an outlook of psychological safety; the courage to be vulnerable enough to risk making mistakes is one we actively encourage as coaches, flying in the face of the risk management I've just described. Or perhaps not, which reveals how loaded the phrase "fail fast" is. Coming up with an idea, thinking it through, experimenting with it, and discovering it's actually awful is a very effective and empowering way to learn and improve quickly. But taking a coachee's vulnerable state and forcing that into something electronic while remaining intentionally ignorant of how it might hurt them sounds more like abuse than empowerment. If there's no risk of our coachees being adversely impacted by us taking a risk, that's our choice to make. And yet coaching is not a solitary profession, and as the professionals in the relationship it's therefore our responsibility to get informed before making decisions we'll later regret.

The world of technology risk management is broad and complex, with many avenues to get lost down. The Information Systems and Controls Association (ISACA) is a global professional body for technology risk professionals boasting a membership of over 140,000, which has published an enormous range of specialist documents detailing good practice in this area. Their broadest-reaching document, detailing at a high level the enabling processes of the good practice framework COBIT (Control OBjectives for IT)[2], is 230 pages long, four of which simply capture the names of those involved in its creation. This book, therefore, will be barely scratching the surface by design, so it's important that we focus our attention on the principal areas that will make the biggest difference as far as coaching with technology is concerned.

We'll therefore spend the rest of this chapter thinking about the following four broad categories, which form a pleasingly memorable alliteration when designing mature systems. When drawing conclusions around how risky a piece of coachtech is, we should be thinking about:

- Adaptability
- Availability
- Accuracy
- Accessibility.

Adaptability

It's a cliché that the only constant in the modern world is change, but a cursory glance over the technology landscape suggests it is the case – perhaps that beloved acronym BAU needs updating to BEAU: Business Evolving As Usual. Technology systems need to be developed over time, introducing new functionality, correcting errors missed during initial testing, patching security vulnerabilities that have emerged, catching up with other technologies on which there's a dependence, and keeping up with the Joneses, to name but a few. And any time there's change, there's risk.

Risk occurs throughout the lifecycle of a technology asset, whether hardware, software, or the underlying infrastructure. Change begins from the point the decision is made to introduce something new; at a personal level it affects one's behaviour as we desperately try to work out how to use it, invariably discovering along the way that it doesn't quite do what we were led to believe it would in the first place, and then eventually being told that it's due to be phased out now we've gotten used to it. And the more technology there is, the more the risk grows. Legacy systems mixing with constantly changing cutting-edge technology increases the complexity of even the smallest change, snowballing the number of opportunities for things to go wrong.

Technology change is famous in the world of risk management for going over budget, arriving late, not delivering the intended benefits, and introducing unwanted surprises. And even once that hurdle's been crossed and the system's in use, if it isn't updated regularly it doesn't take long to become unusable. There's an inherent risk associated with technology systems, that they've been designed to operate within a particular environment, which has only one guarantee: that environment is going to change.

Failed technology change was actually a big influencing factor in my journey in becoming a coach. Having been parachuted into dozens of failing technology projects as an adviser, I found myself consistently concluding that the failure generally sat with people's behaviour rather than the technology itself. End users, technology support and development teams, and third parties consistently refused to communicate transparently, at times seeming bent on sabotaging the change, even if unconsciously. How many times have you found yourself being optimistically encouraged to celebrate a new, exciting, upgraded ability to lose work, crash a computer, and inexplicably restart?

Relying on a piece of technology to enable us to deliver our best coaching will become an issue if something changes in the wider environment that stops it working, or a change in the way it works knocks us off-kilter during a coaching session. This is the sort of thing we should be thinking about when engaging in coachtech, before it's too late, and the one experiencing the repercussions is our coachee, who rightly expects to be receiving some coaching and not a commentary of our IT issues.

At a practical level, this leads us to one conclusion more than any other: the more technology we use, the more change we will need to be ready to cope with for ourselves and our coachees. At a more technical level, a bigger risk lies in the knock-on effects of change on availability, the next category.

Availability

If you haven't experienced the frustration of trying to watch a TV programme or film and getting a response along the lines of "Please try again later", it's because you don't watch TV online, or are not a human. Given the role it's meant to play in relaxation and entertainment, the stress it induces feels unfair; if only one thing in the day is going to go your way, you want it to be the latest episode of *Taskmaster* accompanied by a bowl of ice cream, and once it's melted there's no going back. The complexity of interactions in "Please try again later" could betray an error occurring at any stage of the process from a drained battery in the remote control, through each piece of hardware in our home, the indescribable array of the internet, and every piece of the media provider's puzzle and their supply chains on the other side. As a user, experiencing an issue that prevents technology from working is often more trouble than it feels it's worth, and a call to customer services that concludes with, "it all looks like it's working from our end" is as helpful as a handbrake in a hot air balloon.

It certainly isn't something that's desirable at any point in a coaching relationship. Reliance on undependable technology will make for ineffective coaching, and it's an unfortunate truth that technology systems can stop working for all sorts of reasons, in spite of resilience measures, with the introduction of a single flaw in the process.

This is important to grasp.

As users, all we want is for the technology to be available when it's time to use it, which given the mobile way in which we operate, could be at any time of the day or night. Given the number of parties involved in any technology interaction, the various pieces of technology involved, their constituent parts, and the interfaces between them, availability to that extent just can't be guaranteed. It requires effective demand management, capacity management, and resilience, response, and recovery planning from every participant in the chain.

The stock answer to this from technology providers tends to be that they are proud to commit to availability targets of "five nines", or 99.999%. At first glance, that seems perfectly reasonable – it works out to a tolerance of about five minutes per year of unexpected downtime – but we hit two problems. Firstly, that doesn't include planned downtime, and significant updates that need a system to be disconnected do happen. Secondly, that's at a per component level – the cumulative chance is higher than we'd like of one bit of the technology we're using failing between us, our coachees, and any technology providers in the equation.

We therefore ought to put effort into thinking through what sort of availability we need from our coachtech. This might lead us to test systems immediately before a coaching session to allow for last-minute changes if necessary. We probably also want to have alternative approaches ready to fall back on that offer the same features without reliance on the same infrastructure.

Accuracy

One of the cornerstones of modern technology is data, a mindboggling amount of which we create on an ongoing basis. Since 2016, the amount of data in the world has multiplied a hundredfold.[3] With technology systems so inherently reliant on data, any error, however insignificant, and introduced by whatever cause, might lead to them suddenly and inexplicably becoming unusable. And potentially even worse, they might remain fully accessible while performing indescribably complicated calculations and confidently reporting results and recommendations that are wrong.

Data accuracy is an issue at every stage in the data management lifecycle, beginning with data capture. User input and data uploads both provide opportunities for inaccuracies to be introduced, including omissions, overwriting of existing data, errors in the source data that are retained as it's imported, and duplication leading to over-reporting.

The data must also remain accurate when viewed. I was once investigating an investment bank, which had consistently reported to the regulator that it was performing a lower value of trades than it had actually carried out. Among other things, the creation of a cache intended to accelerate the processing of data had led to updates to an important source data table not being pulled through. It cost the bank millions of pounds to correct the change, pay a fine to the regulator, and compensate the relevant customers. If at all possible, always view data at its source.

It's also important that data be kept up to date. Some information by its nature will change, such as a foreign exchange rate, and a set of numbers appears just as official whether it's right or wrong. Other data might not change frequently, like a coachee's phone number, but that makes it even easier for it to fall out of date without proactive maintenance. While the data must be changed when it needs to be, it must not be changed when it doesn't. It's far too easy to accidentally paste data into the wrong column in a spreadsheet, or to make a slight change to achieve one narrow objective without realising the knock-on effects it can have on the wider system.

One way data finds itself being changed in a way it shouldn't is as a result of data corruption and other system errors. Technology has limitations, and they tend to sit in the background without making a song and dance about themselves. A system change might corrupt a particular field or an entire data repository, needing a restore from a backup. The biggest problem with this is that the identification of the issue might happen after a significant delay, and as a result the backup restore may lead to the loss of data captured in the meantime. One of the big coaching platforms encountered an issue in late 2020 that required them to restore their data from the moment the issue appeared, three weeks beforehand. Any data entered in that period was therefore lost, including scheduled coaching sessions, coaching notes, coach profiles, and invoice activity.

Finally, a lot of data has a shelf life, and must be deleted when it's no longer valid. A fashion designer I once worked with had a line in their management information packs annotated as "error correction". At some point in the company's history, an additional calculation had been introduced into the sales process based on a tax that was no longer valid, but the data engineer that had programmed it had since left the business. This is particularly alarming in coachtech, because the data is often going to be subject to data privacy laws; more on this below.

A good question to continually ask when accessing a system is: "How do I know the data here is complete and accurate?" It may well be, but given the significance of some of the strategic decisions many leaders make based on data, it's worth being prudent. It's also worth maintaining our own backups of critical information; as convenient as it might be to only have to access one location, that paper notepad has its benefits as well.

Accessibility

Data is what gives modern technology a lot of its power. Some of that data sits semi-permanently "at rest" on a piece of hardware, and some is "in transit", moving from one place to another in the form of an email, voice call, or video stream for example. And it's important that both forms of the data are accessible to the right people, and inaccessible to the wrong people. In a coaching setting, the sensitive nature of what might be discussed, and the fact that confidentiality sits as one of the cornerstones of the coaching profession, makes this particularly important. On an equally practical note, none of us want our video coaching to be interrupted by someone who wasn't invited.

Unauthorised access might occur in all sorts of ways, depending on the technology being used and its environment. For example, we might have user accounts with coaching platforms, which are protected by a password. Someone else might get inappropriate access to our coaching files in any of the following ways just for starters:

- A system administrator could unethically access them; they might need that level of access to provide systems support, but should not abuse those access privileges.

- Another coach's user account might be given access to them by accident; a slight tweak in a data table might cause our records to be mismatched.
- Someone might find out our password and use it to access our accounts, even carrying out activity appearing to be us without our knowledge.
- A cybercriminal could remotely access the system using professional hacking tools.

Considering that confidentiality sits within our definition of what coaching is, it's difficult to overstate the importance of this. If nothing else so far has made us think we ought to be cautious when engaging with technology, this should. And when we think about the number of different pieces of technology we rely on to use that coaching platform, the risk landscape grows beyond comprehension:

- The device we use, such as a smartphone, tablet, or PC, could be stolen or simply seen over our shoulder while reading our coaching notes.
- The operating system of the device could have a security vulnerability; these are rapidly shared among cybercriminals as soon as they are discovered on the **dark web**, and might not be patched for some time.
- The software application we use to access it might have security vulnerabilities that could be exploited by a hacker.
- Data passed across the internet, including everything from mobile data masts and infrastructure, to a combination of wired connections, wireless routers, and telephone or cable lines, could be intercepted through a process known as "sniffing", reading the data while in transit to the platform's servers.
- The internet connections within the data centre in which the platform is hosted and the cables connecting to the server hardware could be physically accessed by a member of staff employed by the data centre or one of its suppliers.
- The servers on which the platform is hosted could be tampered with, such as through the imperceptible plugging in of a USB hard drive that extracts the data, or by one of the users managing it remotely.
- The operating systems, any server management tools in operation, the central application, and data repositories might be subject to hacking attempts.
- Any external interfaces (such as to a social media site or independent data repository), however simple, may multiply the risk profile.

Aside from being sensible (please don't write your password on a sticky note), a solution to most of these is **encryption** of the data, which can happen both when it's in transit and at rest. The data is passed through an algorithm meaning that it can then only be viewed in clear text by someone holding the right encryption key. Any data we can access (say, a coachee's goals, messages, and their video feed) is either not encrypted, or is being unencrypted by a key that we hold (for example, in a cookie downloaded from a website).

Figure 4.2 Simplistic map showing devices involved in connecting to a coaching platform

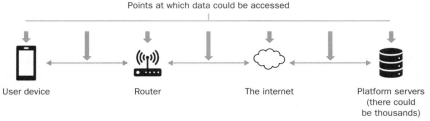

Points at which data could be accessed

User device   Router   The internet   Platform servers
                                                                                         (there could
                                                                                         be thousands)

Unfortunately, encryption isn't as secure as it first appears if only because those who issue us with the keys need to know what the keys are so they can resolve issues. There is such a thing as "zero knowledge encryption",[4] in which the key issuer can't tell what the keys are, so let's start asking for that, if in doubt.

Naturally, the big challenge with all of this is that the extensive chain described above can only ever be as strong as its weakest link. I've seen the world of cybersecurity from the inside, and have seen webcams hacked using an internet search engine, electronic doors in an office being locked via the company website, a bank's unencrypted data feed passing along a cable taped to the outside of a building, and an administrator account for a pension fund shared by more than 150 people. And the more users, locations, pieces of hardware, and interfaces with external systems, the greater the attack surface and the subsequent risk of unauthorised access becomes.

For many coaches, this particular risk is heightened because of those four dreaded letters: GDPR. And despite it applying to all of us, because we all need data that makes a person identifiable (like names and email addresses), only 30% of attendees at a recent ICF webinar admitted to having taken even the first step towards compliance with it.

The EU's General Data Protection Regulation (GDPR) has increased the importance of protecting personal data, and introduced a swathe of specific restrictions. Clocking in at over 55,000 words of legalese, it's easy to feel intimidated by the GDPR, although its governing principles are straightforward enough. An organisation securely holding accurate personal data on someone, with their permission, for a purpose they've agreed to, within the European Economic Area (EEA), and deleting it afterwards, won't get into trouble. An organisation missing any part of that will. The UK applies the GDPR fully through the Data Protection Act, and the penalties for non-compliance can be up to €10 million, or 2% of the organisation's annual global turnover (whichever is higher). The penalties for a breach are double that. So that's 20 million good reasons to want to comply, and possibly the most common form of non-compliance is not registering the fact that you hold personal data with the Information Commissioner's Office. You're welcome.

This is possibly a bigger headache for organisations outside the EEA wanting to access the EU market, which is particularly important for coachtech because several of the most recognisable names are based in the USA. It's more difficult for them because the EU-required controls are not mandated for their supply chain, and many of the approaches intended to streamline the experience, such as the US Department of Commerce's Privacy Shield, have been invalidated.

At this point, it's becoming clear that the only way to protect coachee confidentiality is to eliminate all computing altogether, which in the modern world means meeting exclusively in soundproof Faraday cages! There are ways of reducing the risk of unauthorised access, some of which get awkwardly technical, but once the data exists, it's "out there" and a residual risk will remain. This is one of the most important and difficult subjects to grapple with when thinking about coaching with technology.

There's a lot that can go wrong as far as confidentiality is concerned, and it will cause the biggest headaches if the worst does happen, in terms of reputational, legal, and financial damage. Even forgetting for a moment our professional obligations and simply comparing the weight of data privacy legislation to some of the earlier categories, it would be easy to write them off as barely more than minor inconveniences. Confidentiality should be at the forefront of our minds when engaging with coachtech, even for those of us who are technophiles and find it easy to be swayed by what's newest and shiniest.

TL;DR

Stepping into the world of coachtech introduces new things that can go wrong, and we have a responsibility to understand that in detail and choose how to respond, by knowingly accepting the risks, mitigating them through controls that reduce the impact and/or likelihood of them occurring, or changing our tack to entirely eliminate them. Technology risk categories we should be aware of are:

- *Adaptability* – changes in technology are prevalent and risky, and we should prepare ourselves to cope with that constant change.
- *Availability* – technology will stop working at times, and we should build up our resilience and backup plans to respond to that.
- *Accuracy* – technology relies on data, which can too easily become incomplete or inaccurate. We should elevate our scepticism, always go to the source where possible, and keep our own records to protect against data loss incidents.
- *Accessibility* – confidentiality in technology is essentially impossible, in light of the complexity of end-to-end technology processes. We should exercise an amount of caution commensurate with the consequences of data breaches and our ethical responsibilities as coaches.

Notes

1 The jargon used by risk management professionals is treat (do something), transfer (change the nature of the risk, most commonly through insurance policies), tolerate (accept the risk), terminate (stop the activity presenting the risk altogether). For the purposes of this book, I have not included the transfer element because it risks over-complicating an already technical subject.
2 ISACA (2019) *COBIT*. Available at: https://www.isaca.org/resources/cobit.
3 DOMO (2018) *Data Never Sleeps 6.0*. Available at: https://web-assets.domo.com/blog/wp-content/uploads/2018/06/18-domo-data-never-sleeps-6.png (accessed 17 November 2020); DOMO (2019) *Data Never Sleeps 7.0*. Available at: https://web-assets.domo.com/blog/wp-content/uploads/2019/07/data-never-sleeps-7-896kb.jpg (accessed 17 November 2020); DOMO (2020) *Data Never Sleeps 8.0*. Available at: https://web-assets.domo.com/blog/wp-content/uploads/2020/08/20-data-never-sleeps-8-final-01-Resize.jpg (accessed 17 November 2020).
4 Also known as "end-to-end encryption"; this is not without its own risks, because its introduction allows for bad actors to communicate without surveillance.

5 Ethical quandaries (25 minute read)

Rafael strode into the building, accepting an incoming call as he entered. He was greeted by a soothing voice asking for a mere four minutes to explain how he could transform his productivity through the power of big data. Rafael explained that he would hang up bang on four minutes, and the voice confidently chuckled and said, "I'll make it three."

"Our approach is straightforward but intricate" the voice continued. "One blanket approval from you, and we can access every data stream we need, from your social media to your utilities, calendar, banking, shopping, investments, you name it. We use the most advanced algorithms in the world, which immediately start coaching you in how to start living smarter."

The insider trading fresh on his mind, Rafael asked about security.

"I understand" the voice replied with no hesitation. "We're ISO:27001 compliant and wrap your entire user experience in an encrypted tunnel, meaning only you can see anything. If that's a particular concern, we can add multifactor authentication for no extra cost. Well, I say no extra cost. For no cost at all, actually. We're so confident in our product, we refuse to charge our clients until they've used us for three months, because we want our payment to be a gift of gratitude rather than a transaction. In three months, if you've not got in touch to thank us, your approval will automatically be revoked, and you won't have spent a penny."

Rafael had reached his office by this point and was stumped. Used to batting away salespeople, he'd not seen this tactic before.

"Alright then" he said. "You've won me over. Well done. Send the forms my way."

Emergent ethics

New technology can feel scary. The unfamiliar always carries with it an air of threat, and as technology increasingly hides its workings behind the irresistible sheen of increased productivity or convenient entertainment, its osmosis into our everyday lives can bring with it a sense of unease triggered by how opaque it feels.

The ethical impact of embracing coachtech is a known unknown, which at times can feel like stepping into a hypothetical science fiction universe in which to explore ethical dilemmas. What should a robot coach do if a coachee states an initial goal of hiding the evidence of a crime?

These sorts of discussions can become mind-bendingly fascinating, and are helpful in predicting certain ethical dilemmas. Unfortunately, they're not the way most ethical issues are identified in technology. Most often, we only encounter them after it's too late, because the idea of skirting too close to an ethical boundary simply didn't occur until it became an option. This means that measures to prevent unethical behaviour will always by necessity lag behind that behaviour occurring. For example, digital piracy, while clearly unethical, couldn't be prevented until the technology to share files existed, because prior to that point it didn't need to be.

This is most concerning at the grandest scale, as these examples demonstrate:

- Google has now been fined more than $8 billion by the EU for being anti-competitive,[1] when the high quality of its service is specifically due to the monopoly it holds. The ethical question of the competitiveness of a global, distributed, and universally accessible repository of as much of the world's data as possible had simply never been asked, and now it's too late.
- Facebook has more users than any country has people, and has dedicated itself to continually developing a product that more than anything else addicts those users to it;[2] in principle, that's an issue, but in practice, what to do about it is still very much an open question.
- A 2018 study by the Massachusetts Institute of Technology concluded that fake statements spread six times faster on Twitter than truthful ones, mainly because lies were shared 70% more of the time than the truth.[3]
- Tinder, the dating app which only matches you with people who have already shown an interest, removes the experience of initial rejection from the courting process. The greater ramifications of that on individuals' characters and society as a whole are currently not known.

We can try to predict potential ethical issues that will emerge as coachtech continues to expand, but it's a fact of life that there will be points at which we all notice what has happened around us, and regret not having stepped in sooner to prevent it. For example, it's been noted that when we interact with others in cyberspace, most people experience the online disinhibition effect, self-disclosing and trusting others more than we do in person.[4] These might sound like helpful factors in a coaching setting, but as this seems to be a live experiment filled with unknowns in which the guinea pigs are the entire human race, we simply don't know whether they're toxic or benign.[5]

This is an invitation to us to remain conscious of ethical practices in coachtech. It's also a clear opportunity for us as individual coaches to form an unambiguous baseline of ethical principles that we suspect technology may intersect, which we will hold ourselves personally to account to, and which we will engage with to the extent we can in order to protect our profession.

It's possible to do that, despite the fact that it can feel like technology is running away from us. Concerns about data privacy seem to be hitting the headlines now more than ever, with incidents like the Cambridge Analytica scandal and others, but these are not new. More than forty years ago, a principal for Touche Ross (now Deloitte) said in relation to the increasing use of computing: "A serious question faces our society today: Can it guarantee each citizen's constitutional right to privacy, given the magnitude of information that is routinely collected in the files of both government and business?"[6] Might we collectively be in a better place had we simply paid attention to the concerns that were raised all that time ago? Let's acknowledge our responsibility as change agents, and do something that makes the coaches in forty years' time look at us in joy and gratitude.

This might feel like an additional burden to be carrying while we are already weighed down with so much. It feels like technology companies should be developing products that are transparently and unarguably ethical without us having to pick up that load; the argument used by Mark Zuckerberg, CEO of Facebook, that users should be able to recognise fake news, doesn't resonate. And yet, I believe that the idea that it's the technology providers' fault doesn't reduce our duty to use whatever influence we have to make a positive difference. We are each shaping the world of the future through our words and actions.

Transparency enables better decisions

Our own ethical contexts are formed by nature and nurture, which leads us to react instinctively to ethical dilemmas. We can't help believing that our own worldview is correct, causing a sense of cognitive dissonance at times as we do things that we wish we wouldn't for all manner of reasons, from fear and hunger to peer pressure and lethargy. When it comes to coachtech, our behaviours are more important than our beliefs, because they may affect other people. As a result, our natural approach to treading a fine ethical line, whether prudent caution, reasoned control, excitable experimentation, or carefree adventurousness, will play a part in the way we engage.

Bearing this in mind, it's important that we only embrace coachtech that gives us confidence that we're not going to experience an existential sense of buyer's remorse through crossing an ethical line we didn't realise was there. We should be encouraging innovation, while questioning it at the same time, and the best way to do that is to insist on transparency from every perspective.

That means transparency about finances, because when we can follow the money we can see where the biggest influences are coming from. If those influences are not driving towards increased benefits for coachees, we have a problem. As Daniel Pink put it, "When the profit motive gets unmoored from the purpose motive, bad things happen."[7] An offer of free access to a platform means that others will be paying for our access, which one could argue is inappropriate in a setting that should be empowering a coachee in a non-directive way. And if the user's data will be used to improve the product, shouldn't the provider be paying them for their valuable service?

Similarly, transparency about a technology's inner workings, while sometimes frustrating when you're just trying to get it to work, goes a long way to clarifying its intended purpose and appropriateness for use in a coaching context. As a self-confessed nerd, I'm unashamed of the warm, fuzzy feeling I get when a new mobile app clearly communicates why it's about to ask for certain permissions such as my GPS location. I find some technology companies' hunger for more personal data disturbing, despite – perhaps due to – understanding the underlying reasons for it, and on more than one occasion have refused to engage with a product specifically because I couldn't associate what was happening behind the scenes with my user experience.

Existing standards

The exponential growth of technology in every sector has led those with a philosophical bent to debate the ethical questions that should be considered at a general level. As a result, a huge amount of thought has been put towards the ethical dilemmas presented by technology and how they can be addressed. In 2019, AlgorithmWatch launched the *Artificial Intelligence Ethics Guidelines Global Inventory*,[8] for example, compiling more than 160 good practice frameworks and guidelines only dealing with the development of AI.

This is just scratching the surface of every sort of technology we might interact with as coaches, so that can feel like a lot of responsibility to carry. There's currently no escaping the ethical challenges of technology, but there might be some options that offer more efficient approaches, by outsourcing some of the thinking back to the technology providers. We could insist on approaches like the Trustmark for **Internet of Things (IoT)** devices did in its pilot. The Trustmark provided a free certification for the IoT product if it fulfilled the Trustable Technology requirements around Privacy & Data Practices, Transparency, Security, Stability, and Openness.[9] Other products could undergo an independent audit to offer a level of comfort that certain principles have been in place throughout the development and are embedded into the design, based on good practice such as the Open Data Institute's Data Ethics Canvas.[10]

In addition to any independent assurance, we could use these standards, the principles highlighted in this book, and our own intuition, to engage directly with the provider, asking pointed and thought-provoking open questions like the good coaches we are, such as:

- How would this piece of technology affect the relationship between two friends who became users?
- What would be the indicators of someone using this too much, and what would the impact of that be?
- In a worst case scenario, how could someone intentionally misuse this or its data?

The coachtech we should be most cautious about is simultaneously that which offers the most benefit to the various stakeholders in play. 3D printers are a truly disruptive innovation that puts the power of manufacturing directly into the hands of the consumer. It's not hard to imagine the potential impact it could have on industry, eliminating the need for certain manufacturing jobs and creating more employment in the world of product design, but the idea that someone would print a working gun caught some by surprise, despite in hindsight gun owners and advocates clearly already existing in the populations of 3D designers. What's particularly important to note from this is that the 3D printer manufacturers continue to provide them, considering this an unimportant footnote to accompany the headline story that it's now possible to manufacture a personalised chess set at home.

Similarly, the most disruptive coachtech will offer significant benefits to stakeholders. The most obvious example of these would be robot coaches that could fully replace humans, which would save a huge amount of money for coaching sponsors, and yet would present ethical concerns that could unravel the entire practice of coaching. We'll revisit this in more detail in Chapter 11.

A coaching technology ethics toolkit

Taking into account everything we've just discussed, we ought to consider four big presuppositions when it comes to coachtech.

Firstly, all stakeholders should be engaged in deciding where the ethical boundaries should lie. That includes at least us as coaches, our coachees, coaching sponsors, and professional bodies. It also includes software developers, data scientists, user experience designers, and AI trainers, and will work itself out at three levels:

- At a systemic level, we should agree principles that all coachtech will operate from.
- At a coachtech product level, we should agree scope boundaries using a form of meta-contracting.
- At an engagement level, we should explain what coachtech is in use with our coachees, and what that might mean. The coaching environment, including its technology, should be co-created with our coachees and not forced upon them; coachtech without an opt out will undermine the trust our profession is built on.

Secondly, the purpose of the technology should be unarguably ethical. The technology industry generated the wealth of seven of the ten richest people in the world, meaning that those who set their sights on profit for profit's sake are likely to operate in this space. The purpose of coachtech should always primarily be to enhance coaching practice, through the benefits we discussed in Chapter 3.

Thirdly, ethical principles should be universal and flexibly applicable. That means they should be valid for both technology and coaching as a whole, broad enough that they are flexible to respond to new and changing technologies, and practical enough to not exist purely in a theoretical state.

Fourthly, education, intentions, and actions are equally important. Common technology governance practice is to introduce checklists and certificates that give a potentially false sense of assurance that everything is under control through Campbell's Law: a metric distorting the process it's meant to monitor. It's much better if everyone is empowered to question, understand, and make informed decisions on how to engage, without undermining the importance of the actions themselves. If this means coaches get a basic understanding of what happens when a firewall port is opened, and technology providers pick up foundational coaching principles, that's probably not a bad thing.

Ethical embracing

Having considered everything we've discussed so far and started to apply it in our minds to our coaching practice, it may have occurred to you that the wisest course of action is to avoid technology altogether. The ethical quandaries we might put ourselves in, not to mention the risks we and our coachees are exposed to, make a good case for intentionally becoming a Luddite. That misses the fundamental ethical landscape of coachtech, however. From a purely ethical perspective, our decision-making ought to come down to three sorts of boundaries:

- Some ethical boundaries shouldn't be crossed under any circumstances because as professional coaches we subscribe to a code of ethics.
- Some ethical boundaries we might choose to hold ourselves to for personal reasons, in which case we ought to expect others to respect those decisions, and be gracious with others when our personal stances differ.
- Some ethical boundaries we can give ourselves permission to cross with a clear conscience.

Alright, I lied, there's actually a fourth type of ethical boundary. Our heart in coaching ought to always be for the good of our coachee and the achievement of the objectives of the coaching engagement. It can feel tempting to treat technology as something "other" than coaching, potentially watering it down, and at times even threatening its objectives. Without digging into details on a particular piece of technology, however, it's not at all obvious that's the case. And if we can't unequivocally say that's the case, it might be reasonable to suggest that precisely the opposite is.

If a piece of technology enables identical outcomes to coaching delivered without it but at a lower price, knowingly withholding the technology from the coachee is wrong. Where technology offers opportunities to better achieve positive outcomes from coaching, with an acceptable and transparently understood level of risk, and at a price that justifies it, it would be ethically wrong not to embrace it fully. In other words, we have an ethical responsibility to our coachees to remain informed of coachtech so that we can propose the use of certain technologies to enhance our coaching delivery.

The biggest tension therefore comes with identifying precisely which ethical considerations are being traded off. While understanding the abstract principle that benefits should outweigh costs and risk without overstepping ethical boundaries, in a profession where the greatest difference is in changes of worldview and unstated (and even unconscious) assumptions, those benefits are not always tangible. What should our default ethical stance be towards using technology when the weighing scales haven't clearly tipped the balance?

To an extent, this decision will often be made for us; if a coachee is particularly keen on engaging with a specific technology product, or if a coaching sponsor insists on coaching being delivered using certain technology, we ought to feel free to adopt it with a clear conscience. Underlying that perhaps *laissez faire* attitude, however, ought to be a strong set of principles based around what this chapter has all been about. Regardless of the amount of pressure being put on us by a coachee or anyone else, our handling of ethical issues will always have a greater impact than we realise, giving us reasons to be grateful with the benefit of hindsight, opening the door for more fulfilling opportunities in time, and catalysing system-wide trends in directions we can be pleased about.

If in doubt, let's return to the heart of coaching. The power we hold is dependent more on us as humans than on anything else, and if we're unsure about the full range of effects introducing a particular piece of coachtech will have, exercising caution feels wise. When we embrace technology due to a considered business case that reflects our coachees' best interests and the protection of the future of the profession, we will stand out for the right reasons in a world that can feel at times like it's led more by what's shiniest than what's right.

TL;DR

Ethics in technology are a challenge because it's often unclear what the ethical issues are until it's too late. As a result, thinking through an appropriate ethical stance is important. We each begin with personal approaches to ethics that incorporate our attitudes and actions; increasing transparency over a technology product's business model and technical operations gives us more confidence to engage with it.

Several ethical standards exist over technology, including independent certificates and audits. Drawing from these, we ought to adopt the following presuppositions:

- all stakeholders should be engaged
- the purpose of the technology should be unarguably ethical
- ethical principles should be universal and flexibly applicable
- education, intentions, and actions are equally important.

When we become aware of a piece of technology that would offer benefits without increasing risks or crossing ethical boundaries, we have an ethical responsibility to embrace it fully. And when the ethical impacts are not clear, we should exercise caution and return to the human foundations of coaching.

Notes

1 Chee, F.Y. (2020) EU throws new rule book at Google, tech giants in competition search, *Reuters Technology News*, 1 July. Available at: https://www.reuters.com/article/us-europe-tech-google-antitrust-analysis-idUSKBN242623 (accessed 2 October 2020).

2 Duggins, A. (2020) Why The Social Dilemma is the most important documentary of our times, *The Independent*, 18 September. Available at: https://www.independent.co.uk/arts-entertainment/films/features/social-dilemma-netflix-film-media-facebook-twitter-algorithm-addiction-conspiracy-b454736.html (accessed 2 October 2020).

3 Stokel-Walker, C. (2018) Fake news travels six times faster than the truth on Twitter, *New Scientist*, 8 March. Available at: https://www.newscientist.com/article/2163226-fake-news-travels-six-times-faster-than-the-truth-on-twitter/#ixzz6Zj4yjDJG (accessed 2 October 2020).

4 Lucas, G.M., Gratch, J., King, A. and Morency, L.-P. (2014) It's only a computer: Virtual humans increase willingness to disclose, *Computers in Human Behavior*, 37: 94–100.

5 Lapidot-Lefler, N. and Barak, A. (2015) The benign online disinhibition effect: Could situational factors induce self-disclosure and prosocial behaviors?, *Cyberpsychology: Journal of Psychosocial Research on Cyberspace*, 9 (2): article 3. Available at: https://doi.org/10.5817/CP2015-2-3.

6 Donald R. Wood, quoted in Bannister, C., Sniderman, B. and Buckley, N. (2020) Ethical tech: Making ethics a priority in today's digital organization, *Deloitte Review*, issue 26, January. Available at: https://www2.deloitte.com/content/dam/insights/us/articles/6289_ethical-tech/DI_DR26-Ethical-tech.pdf (accessed 19 October 2020).

7 Pink, D. (2009) *Drive: The Surprising Truth about What Motivates Us*, New York: Riverhead.

8 AlgorithmWatch (2019) *Artificial Intelligence Ethics Guidelines Global Inventory* [blog]. Available at: https://algorithmwatch.org/en/launch-of-our-ai-ethics-guidelines-global-inventory/.

9 The Trustmark completed its pilot in July 2020 and is no longer available, but the categories identified here proved effective measures.

10 Open Data Institute (2019) *Data Ethics Canvas*. Available at: https://theodi.org/wp-content/uploads/2019/07/ODI-Data-Ethics-Canvas-2019-05.pdf (accessed 5 October 2020).

Part 2

The Coaching Technology Landscape

6 Breakdown of the coaching lifecycle (15 minute read)

Flic had left the too-clean meeting room behind her and had spent the rest of the day in coaching supervision and writing a newsletter. She was slicing some bread in the kitchen when a notification appeared off to one side.

She pulled it into view and her heart sank. Coaching was a tough market to be in – for every positive sales session there were a hundred that led to nothing, and losing a client hurt Flic more than yet another rejection text.

Flic had enjoyed working with Rafael. He was interesting, and influential. He was an encouraging client, always willing to try new things and question his assumptions. And now he had fired Flic in a text message, replacing her with a cheaper, process-heavy, inhuman thing.

Flic paused for a moment to steady herself. She had other clients, and he paid towards the lower end of her fee range, but she was sad to be losing the relationship.

She allowed herself the feeling for a few moments, noticing its effect on her, before spending a moment in gratitude for what they'd had together.

Introduction to Part 2

Our interactions with the world as a whole are reflected in the microcosm of our personal coaching ecosystems, and technology is an integral part of it. I often find it tempting when asked to think about my coaching to immediately narrow into the minutiae of the coaching conversations themselves, and yet our roles as coaches extend far more broadly than that. How much attention do we pay to how coach-like we act in contexts other than a coaching conversation? This is one of those dichotomies that it's important to sit with the tension of, and come to a conclusion for ourselves; is it possible that the efficacy of our coaching conversations is bolstered or undermined by the way we interact with a coachee in a pre-sales context?

With this backdrop in mind, let's return to the thought that technology replaces humans – or, at least, human activity. Some of our activity we will instantly place firmly within the bounds of coaching (such as showing intuition in a coaching conversation), while others we might not (such as trying to find a mutually convenient time to meet). As technology becomes more ubiquitous, the line that defines the boundary around coaching activity will close in on us, and we may not realise it's happening. When thinking about the ways that technology interacts with coaching, I find myself getting most excited about how coaching conversations will benefit from it, and yet it's important to start from a broader perspective. This will have two positive effects.

Firstly, the coaching conversations will be enhanced through good use of appropriate technology operated outside of them. Ignoring the effect of that is actually dangerous, as we'll go on to see. Secondly, we all already use a certain level of technology both within and outside of coaching conversations, and we could all be encouraged to take appropriate steps forward. For some, that might be shifting our coaching conversations into a VR location accompanied by live biofeedback monitoring, while for others that might be to tighten up the security controls we operate around instant messaging.

The remaining chapters in this part will explore each of the areas of activity within the entire coaching ecosystem, recognising how some technologies stretch their scopes as we move from one setting to another. As we go through each chapter, we will see increasingly coach-like behaviour being replaced by technology until you and I find ourselves removed from the picture altogether. As a result, the next chapter in particular talks about technology that isn't coachtech *per se*, but rather general technology used by coaches. This is still important for us to reflect on, as we'll see; it can sometimes be difficult to differentiate between coaching-related activities supported by technology, and coaching activities caused as a result of technology's presence.

Administration and productivity

Our coaching practice relies to a certain extent on our ability to lead and manage ourselves well. This includes communicating with stakeholders, managing our diaries, maintaining notes, and general goal and task management. Some of the technology products available to support us in this endeavour apply to any sort of discipline, and as such are much more mature than any products specific to coaching, simply because they've had the time to embed and the investment to be improved. Even for those of us who use very little technology, this chapter is likely to be the most immediately applicable, and it's important to recognise even these more generic tools (like email) as part of the coachtech landscape.

The principles we will have as front of mind in other areas ought also to be applied here, because we ought to hold ourselves to those standards consistently, and our clients almost certainly do. For example, if we would reject the use of a particular coaching model app because the data is not held securely, that same yardstick should be used to judge the appropriateness of a messaging tool we use to interact with our clients. It might feel tempting to skip this chapter because it feels less like coaching – we use these pieces of technology every day without thinking! And that's the issue really; any time we catch ourselves doing something without thinking, we ought to consciously stop to reflect.

Coaching management and oversight

Coaching relationships can be difficult to keep track of, from the first time we introduce ourselves to a client or prospect through to initiating a coaching engagement and keeping on track of it throughout its lifecycle. It's always good to be confident about how many sessions have taken place with a particular coachee, how closely we've been sticking to the original brief, as well as taking a bigger picture perspective on what a coaching journey typically looks like for us. Coaching management tools help us with the day-to-day management of our coaching engagements, as well as providing appropriate information to interested stakeholders. In terms of growth areas for coachtech and what will add the most value over the shortest timeframe, products sitting within this category are likely to be the most disruptive influence. In the longer term, they're likely to be the driving force behind some of the most concerning aspects of coachtech, and so understanding their capabilities is an important knowledge area for us to build on.

Data gathering and analytics

All modern technology is capable of its wonders due to the data it has access to. Despite its serious nerdy connotations, this aligns to coaching more closely than we might realise; as Nancy Kline puts it, "accurate and full information provides the path to good independent thinking".[1] Thanks to traditional coaching inputs such as 360-degree feedback and psychometrics, as well as more emergent technologies like wearables and nanobiotechnology, we can enhance our coaching and seamlessly integrate evidenced insights into our coaching practice. We can also optimise data analytics in the form of push notifications, to reinforce the learnings in coaching sessions through increasing coachees' awareness when they have returned to the day-to-day.

Coaching conversations

Finally, we will reach traditional, in-person coaching conversations, adapted or augmented with various technologies to enhance their delivery. This will include everything from remote coaching in various forms, to coaching methods that are only available with technology, and cutting-edge products that might fundamentally change the way we perceive a coaching conversation to be able to take place. Thoughtfully experimenting in our minds with some of these tools will help us to understand how we might increase the impact of our coaching, while remaining mindful of how changes in mode may shift the purposes and practices of coaching.

Robot coaches

Some coachtech is going to sit squarely in the space of replacing the role of a human coach. Depending on our own circumstances, this will have a clear impact on us personally, will certainly change the role we play in a coaching context, and will have a broader impact on our profession as a whole, so it's worth paying attention to. Most people instinctively consider change to be loss, so we ought to recognise that and reflect on this area in an informed way. In some cases, the introduction of robot coaches may eliminate any justification we have for delivering coaching activities – a distressing thought if you're anything like me and truly enjoy the act of coaching. That said, it may give us permission to experiment more bravely with coaching and with technology than we would have done otherwise.

The questions to answer

As we touched on throughout Part 1, any technology we engage with as coaches is going to be intersecting with four aspects of our coaching practice:

- *Our definition of coaching.* Different technology products might bolster or weaken our ability to deliver coaching in its purest sense. Reminding ourselves of our purpose and being curious about what the impact of various technologies might be, will empower us to make better decisions around which elements of coachtech we will engage with, and what role we will allow them to play.
- *Benefits offered by the technology, and their recipients.* Every piece of coachtech we encounter will provide benefits – that's the nature of technology. Identifying precisely what those benefits are, and who will be receiving them, will increase our awareness of the impact of using the technology, giving us an informed ability to apply it in the areas that will generate the best return on investment (ROI).
- *Risks we are exposing ourselves and our coachees to.* Technology has a big impact on our risk profile, increasing some risks, introducing new ones, and mitigating others. The simple opportunity to think this through allows us to make decisions with our eyes wide open, taking calculated risks that are appropriate for those who will be most affected by their crystallisation. As that is generally going to mean our coachees, for whom we have a duty of

care, it's difficult to overstate the importance of considering risks when engaging with new technology and on an ongoing basis.

- *Ethical concerns presented by technology.* We all want to be doing the right thing, and exactly what that is can be difficult to discern sometimes. This is exacerbated through the introduction of rapidly developing technology, because the ethical concerns might not come to light until the ship has already sailed. Intentionally thinking this through gives us an empowering option to engage with technology with a confidence that we're doing the right thing, rather than putting ourselves in a position we'll regret or acting overly cautiously with a mindset motivated by fear.

TL;DR

The next chapters are going to explore the following categories of coachtech:

- Administration and productivity
- Coaching management and oversight
- Data gathering and analytics
- Coaching conversations
- Robot coaches.

The thoughts we ought to have buzzing around our heads as we are reflecting on these areas ought to include:

- How coachtech will interact with the very definition of what coaching is
- What benefits coachtech offers, and to whom
- How the use of coachtech might affect our risk profiles, and those of our coachees
- What ethical dilemmas we might be presented with through using – or not using – coachtech.

Note

1 Time To Think (2020) *The Ten Components*. Available at: https://www.timetothink.com/thinking-environment/the-ten-components/ (accessed 7 October 2020).

7

Administration and productivity (25 minute read)

Before she had time to fully process what had just happened, a notification shade appeared reminding her to check her email. Finding a comfortable chair to sit in, she sent a thought indicating that she was ready, and her vision blurred to reveal her inbox.

Like the professional that she was, she processed the entire inbox within fifteen minutes, at a glance deleting everything not needing action, and quickly replying to those she could manage. She sent the rest to her productivity platform, tagging each with a context as it went – this one "to do", this one "to read", and this one "at home".

The audio and video snippets sent by contacts on the move could have taken longer, but the tool that transcribed and summarised them for her meant they had been processed already. The rewarding zero appeared in her inbox and Flic switched to a view of her productivity platform to see what needed to happen today.

Getting things done

Humans are experts at making life more complicated than it needs to be. Our minds and bodies are often in tension as we unconsciously pursue the highest levels of Maslow's hierarchy while having no biological need to whatsoever. Just as often, our minds are in tension with themselves as we entirely fail to do what we want to do through having chosen to procrastinate. And we currently live in a world so inescapably complex that the pace of change at times can feel unbearably wearing.

All of us recognise our need for assistance in this area, and our species has done a good job at defining a way to deal with the day-to-day through technology. Some of the everyday technology products, often called "solutions" yet in many cases causing their own set of problems, envelop us on every side, and so we have a responsibility to deal with them well.

The technologies we're about to explore are not all unique to coaching. They're like a gateway drug, making it possible to become more effective and efficient, and enabling us to engage with the world, while forcing us to step into the world of technology. Broadly speaking, the tools we will look at will fall into the following categories:

- Communications
- Web presence
- Personal productivity
- Continuing professional development
- Information storage.

Communications

Coaching is a relational activity. We've spoken about some of the stakeholders involved, and it's important for us to be in touch when necessary with all of them.

Email

The default form of communication in the modern world is email, that bland and ubiquitous mechanism that has become our primary identifier in many interactions. Given the range of alternative methods of communication out there, it's tempting to think that email usage should be going down, but this is hardly the case. In 2015, email traffic was predicted to grow to 246.5 billion emails per year in 2019, an increase of 19%.[1] By 2020, email traffic had grown to such an extent that the prediction for 2024 sat at 361.6 billion, a ten-year increase of 76%.[2] Email tools are becoming more intelligent and more helpful, expanding now to become much broader than simply a faster version of "snail mail".

It's very difficult to imagine operating as a coach without the use of email, and we ought therefore to formally consider it part of our coachtech toolkit. It has settled itself into the centre of gravity for communications, and no other communications tool looks set to upset it yet, thanks mainly to its peripheral functions. Despite their immense power, some of us might underuse our email systems, so maybe an action to take from this book is to revisit that functionality before we branch out into the bleeding edge of innovation. Alongside the sending and receiving of email, most of the big email clients offer:

- a calendar, which we then use as our only scheduling agent
- advanced filing and searching functions for communications and documents
- a contact details database, which tends to synchronise across devices and applications
- a tasks list, which we'll revisit below.

Email brings challenges with it, one of which is its impact on personal productivity. As with many things, often pushed to the extreme with some technologies as we'll go on to see, its strength is its weakness. The fact that anyone with access to our email address has the ability to hurl anything they like onto our screen does a great job of creating opportunities for distraction. On top of that, the additional functionality can lead to it dominating our technology experience, needing to be left open for our calendar to support us throughout the day, and filling our screens and speakers with notifications until we turn them off (that's another action to take, by the way).

And then, the important topic of confidentiality raises its head, because several things can go wrong:

- A typo can cause an email to be sent to the wrong person. If it contains personal or sensitive information, that could have significant ramifications.
- Emails that leave your mailbox travel by default in an unencrypted form, meaning that anyone who intercepts them in cyberspace doesn't even have to put effort into trying to read it, as it appears in clear text. In practice, this means that a summary of a coaching session emailed by a coachee is the virtual equivalent of leaving that printed page on public transport, only it's potentially accessible by the whole world.
- Email systems, like all systems, need to be maintained, and by the nature of the role those who perform that maintenance need to have elevated levels of access, which includes the ability to read emails in one's mailbox. If we're serious about confidentiality – and we should be – the only information we should really share by email should be that which we'd be happy being made public.

Social media

One of the most powerful driving forces of the twenty-first century has been social media. Nearly 4 billion people now use social media,[3] with Facebook alone boasting 2.7 billion users,[4] suggesting that Mark Zuckerberg has influence directly into the eyes of a staggering proportion of the planet – and that's even more terrifying when we consider the other channels that Facebook itself owns.

Do we have the option not to engage with social media? Its benefits are self-evident, providing us with unique access to people unparalleled at any point in history. Some of the most public and influential people in the world have social media accounts, highlighting the intimate ability of every user to attract attention in a way that would have been unthinkable a generation ago. At a more mundane level, I've made friends on social media purely based around a shared appreciation for interactive fiction. For an independent coach with a need to sell their services, social media provides a channel through which we can directly approach a large number of potential buyers in an unimaginably short period of time. It's also a means for coaching authorities to provide content to their followers, such as through memorable images, videos, and other content uploaded directly to the platform, and encouraging attendee interaction for online events.

As potential expands, so do the risks, and social media is a topic generally presented as negative in every context other than from the perspective of digital marketing. The power of social media lies in the data it holds, and data in an online system is essentially undeletable. How many times has the phrase "such and such has since deleted the tweet" appeared in a news story, followed immediately by the tweet in question verbatim? One single post, perhaps intended to be private, perhaps reliant on various safeguards, perhaps published early by mistake, could damage a coach–coachee relationship forever, along with the reputation of the coach, and at times the coaching profession as a whole.

And all of this is without mentioning the addictive nature of social media, which has been widely reported and is indicative of perhaps the biggest risk associated with modern technology: its tendency to run away from us faster than our ability to manage it can keep up. At present, the only ways social media are regulated are those ways that apply to everything, which is unhelpful when the subject at hand didn't exist when the regulations were formed.

Instant messaging

Where social media is a loudhailer designed to broadcast information, instant messaging is a yoghurt pot on a piece of string, offering the ability to target it at specific people. At a fundamental level, instant messaging tools do the same thing that email does but with a different user experience. From that perspective, the temptation could be to want to simplify life and uninstall everything apart from email, but we hit the biggest problem that technology has encountered from the moment it was introduced until now and shows no sign of stopping: its interaction with people. In what Seth Godin calls the *Connection Economy*,[5] sometimes the only reason we engage with certain technologies is that the disbenefits of not using them outweigh the hassle of allowing ourselves to get caught up.

To differentiate instant messaging from email, we might want to consider it predominantly synchronous text-based communication, while email is predominantly asynchronous. It's possible to have an email sitting in one's inbox for weeks, while instant messages as a general rule are dealt with much more quickly. They're different at a technical level as well. One advantage that some – not all – instant messaging tools have over email is zero-knowledge encryption of messages. It's possible now for us to exchange information digitally with a coachee and feel protected against the messaging traffic being sniffed (although the encryption still isn't without its flaws; backups are still accessible by system administrators). That's more secure than email, and particularly when there are no realistic alternatives that eliminate all risk, the combination of convenience and security becomes a big selling point. One important exception to this would be SMS messages, which are never encrypted.

Web presence

The business of creating websites for coaches is booming at the moment. Some of them are, unarguably, works of beauty, with opportunities to subscribe to newsletters, blogs filled to the brim with high-quality thought leadership, overviews of their coaching philosophy and the sorts of products and services they offer, photographs that look like the pages of a high-end fashion magazine, testimonials from coachees whose lives have been changed thanks to their coaching, detailed, interactive life stories, and as many other examples as there are coaches with websites.

Websites exist for several purposes. Coaches' primary purpose for a website tends to be as a virtual shop window to allow potential clients to discover, or validate, their existence. Despite many coaches getting no business directly from their website at all, getting a good website feels like the sort of thing a serious coach needs to do.

As much as a website makes it possible to be found through an internet search engine and to offer a streamlined, integrated ecommerce service, the majority of us get work based on word of mouth. A website feels like a health factor rather than a foundational pillar of a coach's brand management strategy. And yet the risks one faces with a website, through accidentally using someone else's intellectual property, inadvertently disclosing something from a coaching session while creating content, or creating a new hackable space that wouldn't have existed otherwise, seem to shift the balance quite firmly in favour of not having a website unless it's serving a purpose other than coaching (such as for selling other products or services).

A more sensible approach for most coaches would be to have another, hosted location that would contain the same information, without the hassle of managing one's own website. Profile pages in online coaching directories do exactly the same thing, although having too many presents a new risk that one will become out of date and then have the effect of making the coach look out of touch, the precise opposite of the desired impact.

Personal productivity

A lot of coachees, when asked what they want out of coaching, say they want to get better at time management. The world wants us to achieve more in a day than anyone could possibly manage, and most people's own competing priorities exceed that possibility as well. On top of that, the potential for procrastination is so great that at the time I'm writing this, an internet search for "productivity tips" generates about 266 million results, most of which are likely to boil down to something along the lines of "stop spending your time reading articles on how to be more productive". Or, at least, they should do.

The number of technology products out there focused on personal productivity is gargantuan. Some are focused on specific areas of concern, like distraction blockers, plugins that generate suggested replies to emails, and so on. These tend to offer solutions to specific problems, and many tell a compelling story as to why those problems should be solved. In most cases, two general principles hold true:

1 If the problem wasn't obvious before the marketing explained its solution, there's a good chance that solving it will come with undesired side effects.

2   As much as these productivity tools do offer genuine benefits, they some-
    times need a level of discipline for them to work (a notifications blocker
    itself becomes a time-waster if every app needs manually checking several
    times every day). Therefore, for those problems where self-control would
    solve the problem as well as the technology, it's a better use of time to work
    on developing that characteristic rather than trying to outsource it.

Other productivity tools are intended as holistic life-hacks, offering a system
through which we can take control of everything we want to do. These tend to
come with the acronym GTD, which originated from David Allen's excellent
book *Getting Things Done.*[6] His system proposes the maintenance of multiple
lists of actions and information, and technology enables us to implement GTD in
our own lives. Implementations include strict word-for-word applications of the
book, simplistic digital-first approaches, purist "notes only" tools (like the task
lists in email clients), replications of sticky notes on whiteboards, and fully customisable platforms that integrate with email clients, time tracking software,
calendar applications, video communication tools, and **customer relationship
management (CRM) systems**. Some of these have taken GTD to the extreme,
offering GPS-powered triggers that remind you that you need eggs when you're
close to a supermarket, tags that give you multiple views depending on what
context you need them for, gamification and statistics to artificially motivate us
to do what we tell it we want to do, and consumable content designed to inform
us about the psychology of making new habits.
    We do tend to end up trying to keep lots of plates spinning, including actions
we want to perform, coaching processes we want to keep on track, and other
relationships we want to keep warm. GTD tools can therefore be very helpful,
in particular because of their ability to replicate content across multiple devices
in near real-time; a thought occurring while on the move can be captured on
one's phone and is already available at the laptop. Like all technology, they
come with health warnings. For example, the amount of time worth spending
in the tool is always less than the amount saved by using it, confidential data
stored in a GTD tool is just as likely to be accessed as data held anywhere else,
and it's as much use as a chocolate teapot if it unexpectedly becomes
unavailable.

Continuing professional development

Part of the coaching mindset is to continuously remain in an attitude of learning, through personal reflections, engaging in coaching supervision, and maintaining good habits around continuing professional development (CPD). In my
role as coaching supervisor, a question that comes up relatively frequently is
how to source good quality CPD material. The challenge with this is knowing
which of the plethora of internet sources is worth investigating, and so my
encouragement tends to be to jump in the deep end with something unfamiliar
and then to reflect sceptically on it.

Technology gives us all easy access to research papers, blogs, articles, books, video series, mobile apps, and online training courses, to name a few, some of which are absolutely excellent. Even those that aren't, however, can help us to learn if we take that final step to reflect sceptically on what we've just experienced.

The risks around using technology for CPD come from its convenience tending to focus on content delivery more than reflection, discussion, or application. It's possible to get a certificate that validates having played a series of videos, and that isn't the same as actually developing the skill. Good, technology-enabled CPD requires sufficient practical experience of each element, reflection on how we'll change as a result of it (or not – and why not), and, if possible, feedback from someone with more experience.

Information storage

Coaches need to have a way of holding and accessing data, whether we're talking about reference material for coaching models, content we know coachees would benefit from us sharing from time to time, coaching reflection notes, records of training for the purposes of accreditation, or any of a whole range of other potential topics. Nowadays, the word most often connected with information storage is likely to be: "cloud". The idea that a certain piece of information is stored "in the cloud" is often casually tossed around without fully understanding what this means.

All data has to be stored somewhere on a physical device (even so-called "serverless" computing still relies on physical servers to host the data). The concept of cloud computing, while delivered through virtual servers that can change their nature and move from one physical device to another, is essentially the same principle as a file being stored on a physical server in the 1990s. That said, modern technology will typically dynamically hold data in any of a number of server locations depending on various criteria, often in at least two separate locations simultaneously to ensure it remains available even if one connection is lost. The data might also be replicated onto the device you're accessing it from, and it will likely be backed up on a regular basis to yet another location to protect against the loss of too much data in case it's accidentally deleted or corrupted. For those not taking notes, that's at least four different physical locations the data exists in.

File storage and file sharing tools offer various facets of the same core functionality. They're increasingly helpful and accessible. They're also relatively secure, although there's a trade-off that happens between confidentiality and convenience, and a conclusion around that isn't always going to be self-evident. As technology continues to advance and automated processes increasingly enter the picture, such as online invoicing triggered by activity and blockchain-powered contracts, the complexity will make that calculation even more difficult to handle.

TL;DR

Our day-to-day interactions with technology underpin our coaching activity at the broadest level. This includes:

- Communications tools, which we need in order to connect to people and which we should get comfort over as far as confidentiality is concerned
- Our web presence, which arguably needs no more than a comprehensive profile page in a coach directory
- Personal productivity tools, which help us regain control over the myriad priorities we try to juggle yet which need careful thought in terms of their confidentiality and availability
- CPD options, which give us unprecedented levels of content that should challenge our thinking habits, be treated with caution in terms of their evidence base, and be supported by good reflective practice
- Information storage, which is necessary and needs us to be mindful of confidentiality controls.

Notes

1   The Radicati Group, Inc. (2015) *Email Statistics Report, 2015–2019*. Available at: https://www.radicati.com/wp/wp-content/uploads/2015/02/Email-Statistics-Report-2015-2019-Executive-Summary.pdf (accessed 22 September 2020).
2   The Radicati Group, Inc. (2020) *Email Market, 2020–2024*. Available at: https://www.radicati.com/?p=16885 (accessed 22 September 2020).
3   Kemp, S. (2020) More than half of the people on Earth now use social media, *We Are Social* [blog], 21 July. Available at: https://wearesocial.com/blog/2020/07/more-than-half-of-the-people-on-earth-now-use-social-media (accessed 22 September 2020).
4   Vlessing, E. (2020) Facebook tops 2.7 billion monthly active users in latest quarter, *The Hollywood Reporter*, 30 July. Available at: https://www.hollywoodreporter.com/news/facebook-second-quarter-earnings-rise-continued-user-growth-1305161 (accessed 22 September 2020).
5   Godin, S. (2018) *The Connection Economy* [video]. Available at: https://www.youtube.com/watch?v=SB690t8_cpI.
6   Allen, D. (2001) *Getting Things Done*, Harmondsworth: Penguin Books.

8   Coaching management and oversight (34 minute read)

The top item on Flic's to-do list began with a familiar three asterisks, the sign of an urgent and automatically generated action from her coaching platform, reminding her of the first time she connected with Rafael.

Six months earlier, using her eyes and mind to navigate the screen that had appeared in front of her, she had pulled up the item:

***NEW COACHEE – RAFAEL MEJIAS-YEDRA.

Within the body text of the action was a picture of Rafael, his job role and life timeline automatically populated from his social media feeds. Flic quickly got the impression of a shy boy who had stumbled into a job in marketing in his mid-twenties before marrying in his early thirties, divorcing in his late thirties, and switching careers to enter the world of politics. He had moved from public relations to policy development, and only recently had become a Member of Parliament.

The coaching needs analysis had already been processed by the platform to suggest some suitable coaching models, alongside the headline "Fulfilment coaching".

A quick glance at the timing of the first session, and Flic had struggled not to physically flinch as she saw it was only ten minutes away. Her brief panic calmed a little when she remembered the platform wouldn't have booked it were she not free, but that didn't give her the time she would have preferred.

"Fine" she had muttered, a tingle of excitement mixing with the disappointment she still felt, and she had moved swiftly to the kitchen to make a cup of tea.

Controlling the process

The point at which we start looking at technology that exclusively sits in the category of coachtech is when we start thinking about the journey of a coaching process. Regardless of our differing coaching approaches and styles, all of us will tend to follow a similar series of steps as we engage with our coachees, and technology offers the potential to make each one more effective. Given the different stakeholders involved, all of these steps may not be entirely relevant all of the time, but a continual awareness of them helps us understand the wider purpose that the coachtech is serving, and ought therefore to inform our use of them. The steps coaching engagements follow to a greater or lesser extent are:

- Digital marketing
- Management, administration, and quality assurance of coaching engagements
- Setting and validating objectives

Digital marketing

Social media marketing

Marketing nowadays is appallingly simple, which makes it appallingly difficult. Imagine Paul, a friend of mine who used to run a chain of hairdressing salons in the Midlands. He could get an advert onto the screen of specific users based on their age, gender, location, social media activity, and purchasing history. If you were aged 28–33, male, lived within a ten-minute walk of one of his salons, had liked the pages of certain hairdressing products and celebrities, and had paid for a haircut online 4–8 weeks before, an advert would appear in your Facebook feed with that celebrity and those specific products offering a special offer on a haircut right around the corner.

His conversion rate on that advert was astronomically high, and it goes without saying that Facebook would point at this as a good user experience; that user needed a haircut and got one suited to his own preferences. But there are two big problems with this scenario, the full extent of which we may never truly know.

Firstly, Paul's ability to do that was only successful because no-one else had, and he would be the first to admit that it's only a question of ticking the right boxes on the marketing portal. Where we are looking to use social media marketing as a tool for selling our coaching, its ease of use is as much a threat as it is an opportunity. By targeting the precise niche we're pursuing, the marketing content will be seen by the most relevant prospects, who will at the same time have seen every other coach chasing after that same niche. Standing out by being the most relevant is a good way to instil confidence, so what's the best way to do that when the competition is all equally as relevant?

The answer to that question is relatively straightforward, which brings us to the second big problem. The only way to become more successful when the target market is continually seeing equally good services on offer is to become an expert at marketing, which in the digital age means becoming an expert in manipulation. The reason Paul's haircut marketing was successful was because of the targeted marketing content, not because of the service he was offering. He could have run multiple adverts side-by-side for different age groups and different interests, testing different versions of adverts for different populations and continually tweaking until he was able to almost guarantee their success, without once having the quality of the service he was offering questioned.

When the coaches who get the most business, and as a result end up wielding the most influence, do so only because of their exceptional digital marketing ability, that should give us cause for alarm. In this case, a "coach" whose service is actually providing advice and opinions to individuals could end up being offered more coaching work than the best non-directive coaches, despite their offering not actually being coaching. As someone who wants to protect and improve the reputation of the coaching profession, I find this concerning. When we find ourselves depending more on a skillset outside of that of coaching to succeed, we unearth the chilling truth that social media, in the face of the platitudes of wanting to be helpful and connect people, care less about positive systemic impact than maybe they have led themselves to believe.

Email marketing

A particularly common marketing practice among many coaches is to build an email list, typically in exchange for a free piece of information, like an ebook. Coaches using email marketing tend to send this list a newsletter or article in an email on a periodic basis to remind clients and prospects of their existence, without having to put the effort into sending personal emails to all of them.

At the simplest end of the email marketing spectrum sits the humble spreadsheet filled with contact details, perhaps hosted in one of the online information storage systems we discussed in the last chapter, which can be copied and pasted into the next email when it's time. This is probably sufficient for most of us, so long as we make sure that the email addresses are in the BCC field, to avoid inadvertently sharing personal details and falling foul of GDPR. And that risk is going to be the same whether you're using this simple approach or a whizzy CRM system. Someone who gains access to our spreadsheet or CRM database has the personal details of all of our clients and prospects in one fell swoop.

Email marketing is going to be a core part of some of our roles, and not at all in others. It's an efficient way to continually pop up in people's email inboxes so that our name becomes familiar and therefore trusted, but it isn't very effective at selling coaching services in its own right. Compared with social media marketing in particular, it can feel a bit bland in the modern day if it's being used for that purpose. In addition, plenty of email clients now automatically file marketing emails separately, allowing the recipient to delete them all without reading them, and so our latest reflections on a particular leadership model, for example, end up falling into the same category in the recipient's mind as the endless repetitive emails asking them to book holidays, look at the latest fashion trends, and make the most of a deal on a new perfume.

Coaching platforms

One of the most significant shifts in the coachtech landscape has been the introduction of coaching platforms, which take three forms, generally speaking:

- coaching administration platforms designed for individual coaches to increase their ability to manage coaching engagements
- coaching management platforms designed for organisations to deal with the administration and oversight of a coach pool
- digital coach brokers, acting as an online marketplace to give coachees streamlined access to independent coaches.

At their heart these are different views of the same object, as a coaching management platform simply expands a coaching administration platform's scale, a digital coach broker takes on the administration and oversight of a virtual coach pool, and most coaching management platforms include functionality allowing employees to browse what is essentially a coach marketplace. In many cases, the lines have already become blurred, with some digital coach brokers moving into the world of business-to-business at scale, and some coaching management platforms beginning to expand into the cross-organisation and direct-to-consumer spaces.

The benefits offered by these platforms are made clear when we reflect on how most organisations come to start using coaching. An individual (let's call her Sandy) has a positive view of coaching, and begins to bring it into her organisation. The coaching process followed only exists in any tangible form in Sandy's head, and as the organisation matures and a pool of coaches is developed, the list of coaches ends up there too. When a coachee is identified, Sandy matches a coach based on who she thinks might work well, and contacts them to check if they're available. If Sandy is on top of her administration, she might update a spreadsheet somewhere to record the match.

It might be helpful to think about the maturity of Sandy's environment on a scale from 1 (Ad hoc) to 5 (Optimised). Less mature environments rely heavily on the good knowledge, skill, and discipline of people like Sandy. In most cases, a maturity level of 3 (Defined) would be the minimum to provide comfort that coaching is going to consistently provide value, and 4 (Measurable) is a sensible objective to limit the risks posed by technology.

This is one of the most significant issues faced by leaders of organisational coaching because of the transparency required, particularly when making budget decisions. On paper, coaching can look like an easy cost to cut, because it looks like time and money spent with nothing to show for it. Unlike an activity explicitly driven by customers or regulators, there are no push factors around coaching giving a negative outcome to avoid, and no tangible pull factors giving them a positive outcome to drive towards. Coaching can therefore be perceived as a pleasant, harmless activity, but not something to invest in.

Coaching platforms go some way to addressing this issue, because they force the maturity into at least level 3 (Defined); the platform needs a process to follow by its nature. And because it's a system reliant on data, the capability to assess and quantitively change the process moves from a state of guesswork based on anecdotal evidence and into grounded reality. With that in mind, let's consider the most palpable differences coaching platforms make, beginning with the administration of coach matching.

Figure 8.1 Capability maturity model for coaching with technology

Coach matching sits in stark contrast with the rest of the coaching experience, which can be hugely rewarding for us and our coachees throughout a relationship. In preparation for coaching sessions, the joy of the subject matter offers an intriguing and pleasurable experience. In coaching sessions, "aha" moments are taking place. Immediately following coaching sessions, the breakthroughs of identifying limiting assumptions provide doses of dopamine throughout the day. And even years after a coaching engagement has concluded, some of the learnings that took place remain front of mind for the coachee as they interact with the world.

Compare that with the coach matching experience, which in many cases can feel like a drawn-out, awkward time of little value. When done manually, the process often begins with some sort of coaching needs analysis (CNA) form, and the succinctness and clarity of this isn't guaranteed. Assuming the CNA generates a clear enough output, Sandy will encounter the challenge of finding the right coach based on the coaches' experience and specialisms. More often, however, she will match a coach based on who happens to be on her mind at the time, at which point the conversations around availability and, if relevant, budget approvals can take place. This could be weeks after the CNA was completed, and may only take the coachee as far as initiating chemistry meetings depending on the context. As a result of this lengthy process, most of us have experienced an initial coaching conversation in which either the coachee is unable to remember the precise reason why coaching was initiated, or the circumstances have sufficiently changed to make the CNA no longer relevant.

Coaching platforms have the ability to reimagine a streamlined version of this process, at least for one-to-one coaching. The coach matching is accelerated, its impact is increased, and everyone gets to save valuable time. Instead of an initial conversation about coaching with Sandy, a potential coachee accesses the platform and is immediately greeted by a CNA in the form of some simple questions. The time taken for Sandy to find and send the CNA and the potential coachee's natural procrastination have been removed, so the elapsed time of a week or more has been transformed into a few minutes. The moment the questions are answered in the platform, a few coach profiles appear, whose specialisms align to the CNA output, whose rates are within the tailored budget range, and who have availability. The potential coachee selects one on the spot,

Figure 8.2 A fictitious coach's overview of their engagements in the coaching.com coaching platform

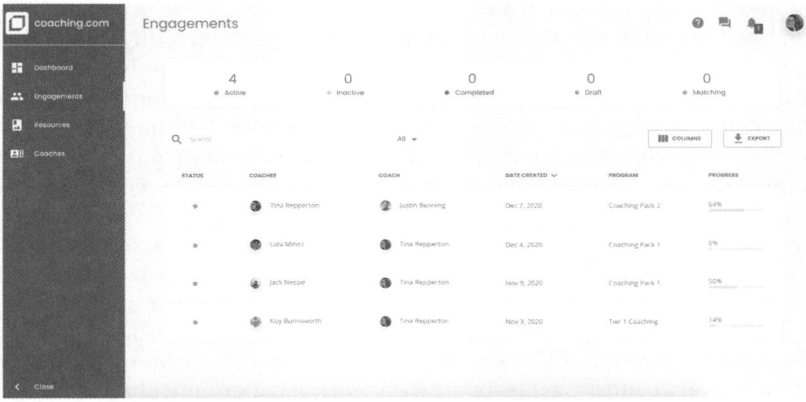

schedules an initial session through the platform's interface with the coach's calendar, and could be receiving a coaching session that same day. And at the other end of the process, when supplier management is built into a platform, we're able to raise a pre-populated invoice automatically, and interface directly with our accounting packages, giving Sandy comfort, and saving us time – she may never have to approve a payment again!

This could look like Sandy has been replaced by a machine, and yet coaching platforms are not a valid reason for job losses, because of the additional roles they create:

- Coaching platforms increase demand for coaches. They make coaching accessible to more people in a more streamlined way, regardless of seniority, referred to as the democratisation of coaching. The ability for potential coachees to browse a marketplace of coaches and self-initiate coaching engagements is an exciting new opportunity that will naturally increase the volume of coaching that takes place.
- Coaching platforms increase demand for strategic coaching roles. They introduce new levels of clarity for insight and oversight, like how many coaching sessions are being booked, which topic areas are the most popular, which coach profiles get the most attention, what patterns there are in rescheduling and cancelling sessions, what themes emerge from coaching objectives, and so on. Where coaching processes have historically been designed based on Sandy's personal preferences, with a coaching platform these can be designed based on what's working best in that context.
- Coaching platforms increase demand for coaching support roles. The data that's gathered can form a basis for more mature quality assurance activity, like validating the accreditation, supervision, and CPD of coaches. It also opens up continuous improvement opportunities, such as through identifying that the majority of coachees are exiting coaching relationships early, leading to updates to the coaching processes.

The value coaching platforms can offer is clear in terms of efficiency, coachee experience, and monitoring ROI. The market leaders are all also extending their capabilities to meet other organisational needs in an integrated, streamlined way. But risks are also present. I was working with a global company that wanted a new coaching platform. The business case was clear, and after an extensive procurement exercise and project to configure it and train everyone, it was rolled out across the coach population. Six months later, the platform was decommissioned. It wasn't providing the anticipated value, and it's a good example of how humans are often the weak link in technology. The coaches weren't updating their availability on the platform, and as a result the equivalent of Sandy in this company was playing the same role as before, only now with another technology system to take into account. This wonder in modern technology, with all the promise of everything digital transformation has to offer, had been implemented and turned into a glorified spreadsheet.

If we don't keep our coach profiles on a coaching platform up to date, we won't be matched with coachees that we'd work most effectively with; both of us will miss out. If the coaching doesn't take place in the platform itself and we don't record when sessions have taken place, the comfort that the platform's dashboard provides is actually false assurance – not giving credit where credit's due, and potentially being more harmful than not knowing what's happening.

The problems don't end there. Any time an activity that fundamentally involves humans – as coaching does – reduces its time and cost, other factors are impacted:

- the scope of what's possible
- the quality with which it's delivered (because the scalability of the most skilled humans is much more finite than that of machines)
- the benefits experienced as a result
- the risks faced.

One of the biggest risks presented by coaching platforms emerges from the amount of data they hold, because the biggest concern of all has to be that of confidentiality. In a particularly vulnerable coaching session with a white man, my coachee said he wanted to discuss unconscious bias. He disclosed his frustration at his perception of a narrative of whites and blacks as perpetrators and victims, and said he wanted the space to fully explore his thoughts without feeling like he'd be judged for saying something that would be considered inappropriate in public. Coaching is the perfect environment for that, and yet if he thought that discussion topic might be included in a corporate report, he might understandably feel hesitant to speak about it for fear of greater ramifications, limiting the capabilities of the coaching.

In a broader sense, a coaching platform will capture which coaches are working with which coachees, and the extent of the data captured may quickly cross the line into inappropriate breaches, however inadvertently. Not to mention the fact that some platforms encourage the taking of notes in the live session, or facilitating candid social media style reflective discussions between a community of coaches. While access to this potentially sensitive data may be restricted at the time, the risk of unauthorised access remains.

Objective setting

Evaluating the impact of coaching is a challenging subject area. Established coaching practice includes objective setting, holding coachees accountable for progress against those, and assessing the downstream impact of a coachee having engaged in the coaching. The EMCC, for example, encourages this to its fullest extent in accredited Senior Practitioners, for whom one of the Capability Indicators is to encourage the coachee to explore the "wider context and impact of desired outcomes".[1] Precisely how this is done remains flexible for us to decide with our coachees, and technology offers some solutions to strengthen and enrich this important component.

At the most basic end of the coachtech spectrum sits the world of templates. Quick-access email templates don't feel like the bleeding edge of innovation, but can save a surprising amount of time, and it's the same with coaching. If a structured series of questions enabled through an online form could help a coachee define their goal using a good practice model, the time available for us to ask deeper questions that potentially add more value could be expanded.

A systemic angle on goal setting is where technology comes into its own. Enabled by automated interfaces to relevant technology systems and databases, an objective-setting tool empowers a coachee to remain in control of setting goals, while demonstrating how the coaching is contributing to a bigger agenda. Within an organisational context this might include the employer's strategic goals or value statements, competence frameworks, or outputs from performance reviews directly extracted from the relevant technology systems. More broadly, it could include values-led frameworks such as the United Nations' Sustainable Development Goals, or established standards for different focus areas like leadership, wellbeing, and diversity & inclusion.

These sorts of interfaces can cause problems, however, as I discovered when I got to visit Google's head office in Mountain View. Landing at the airport, my first port of call was an ATM to withdraw some dollars. Upon putting my debit card in, I was greeted with a message telling me it had been blocked for suspected fraud. I contacted my bank, who said they had identified a suspicious transaction, which turned out to be me, unexpectedly in San Francisco rather than London. I patiently explained that I had called them in advance of leaving the UK, and it turned out that I had only told the credit card team and not the debit card team. Presumably, I should have asked to speak to every other bank employee on the off chance they might also need to know. This frustrating event just highlights how effective technology has become at enabling multiple systems to work in conjunction with one another. I often don't notice this happening, but I certainly do when it doesn't. Regardless of how technically complex the solution within my bank might be, our expectation as customers is that data will be shared seamlessly when it needs to be, and yet that isn't as simple as it sounds, particularly when older technology systems are in use. When setting goals that rely on other systems for context setting and alignment, the chance that the technology systems may not talk to each other precisely how we'd like them to – or at all – should remain front of mind.

Capturing goals can also be helpful for our own reflective practice. Having them all in one consistent data store gives us the benefit of considering the sorts of goals our coachees are setting: What does it say about me as a coach if three-quarters of my coachees set "building executive presence" as a goal? It might say more about the coachees than us, it might reveal a specialism, and it definitely feels like something valuable to take to supervision.

It's not just us who benefit from this wider perspective on coaching goals; data on objectives also helps the coaching sponsor. From their helicopter view, a thematic analysis of coaching topics could act as a trigger for wider organisational development work, such as being confronted by the fact that better work–life balance appears as a goal for every member of the legal team. Perhaps more significantly, tracking the impact of coaching helps to validate the investment being made in it. This throws up a bit of an ethical dilemma. Coaching delivers value and should stand up to scrutiny, and yet opening up that information threatens confidentiality. Would it be right for us to break that confidentiality for the sake of demonstrating its value and expanding its reach?

Against this backdrop, let's not lose sight of the effect goal-setting technology could have for our coachees, who want to make positive changes in the short and long term. Goal-setting tools in a coaching platform built around the Rubicon model of action phases, for example, sit alongside the coaching sessions to provide a helpful wrapper for coachees to set goals, plan their actions, do what they intend, and reflect on their progress. When used alongside an app on the coachee's smartphone for quick reference, this could have deep impacts on the demonstrable effectiveness of coaching sessions, the use of a coachee's time outside of them, and with a more systemic lens as well.

That said, there are some significant downsides to the rigour technology naturally applies to the process of setting goals. A Harvard Business School study described goal setting as "a prescription-strength medication that requires careful dosing, consideration of harmful side effects, and close supervision".[2] Goals need to be able to change and at times be ignored in order for coaching to be as impactful as it can be, and perhaps the most significant negative effect of this sort of technology is its influence on our behaviour as coaches.

The objective-setting technology tools currently available are spreadsheets at heart, however visually appealing the graphical user interface (GUI) is. This gives an implicit preference towards goals that are easily quantifiable, and this provides one particular benefit: it's much simpler to track a number than a feeling. If our priority is to demonstrate the impact coaching is having, "my coachee saved themselves eight hours each week" is much more tangible than "my coachee feels a bit braver". And if our success is being measured on our

Figure 8.3 A report from MyExcelia, an automated coaching ROI platform

Executive Coaching ROI
Final Report

Ripple Effect: Monetary Impact
Eric reported several impacts. Specifically Eric reported that as a result of improving his communication and developing individual members on his team, in addition to developing the team overall, he was able to improve team productivity, engagement and profit margin (Table 1.2).

Area of Impact	Monetary Value
Improve Profit Margin for Team: In a final debrief with Eric to close the coaching engagement, Eric provided input that the profit margin for his team had gone from 5% at the start of coaching to 8% and representing a gain of $315,700. Utilizing his estimation of the amount he believed was due to the impact of coaching, that amount was adjusted to $10,284.	$10,284
Utilization of Team: Additionally, utilization increased from 75% to 80% at the end of coaching and representing $324,000 in profit margin. Again, utilizing Eric's estimation of the amount he believed was due to the impact of coaching, that amount was adjusted to $38,880, totaling $49,164 both moneteary goals improved due to coaching. All financial metrics and values were validated by the Chief Financial Officer who was the sponsor of the coaching client.	$38,880
Improved Employee Engagement: While specific measures were not captured, Eric reported that the level of energy and enthusiasm from the team indicated that employee engagement had lifted.	Not monetized.
TOTAL	$49,164
COSTS	$10,440
ROI	371%

Table 1.2 Financial impact as reported by Eric and verified by Chief Financial Officer of company.

demonstrable impact, we're much more likely to allow the coaching sessions to focus on the former output rather than the latter, even when the more fundamental, sustainable, effective, and pleasing change would be their increased bravery.

One of the most exciting levers that coaching can pull in achieving its greatest levels of impact is that of mindset shifts. They underlie every behaviour that coaching is introduced to affect, so embed change in a much better way, and yet are hard to capture as leading metrics for more tangible behaviour change. Using technology to aid in setting goals brings with it the benefits of clarity, transparency, and an ability to take a bigger picture perspective, but the risk it presents in terms of limiting the efficacy of coaching shouldn't be overlooked in the name of convenience.

TL;DR

As a general rule, coaching processes are highly manual, time-intensive, and reliant on the knowledge of those involved. Technology can assist in coaching marketing, for example through social media marketing and email marketing.

Coaching platforms, including those designed to assist in administration within organisations and digital coach brokers, can accelerate coach matching processes, and provide valuable insight into coaching engagements, offering opportunities for continuous improvement, but increasing the risk of a confidentiality breach.

Other technologies can also be used as plugins to capture high-quality objectives and monitor ROI. This can be helpful in keeping us on track to deliver impact in our coaching, and offers coachees tangible monitoring opportunities, although risks at times narrowing our focus to set granular outcomes at the expense of more flexible and fundamental mindset shifts.

Notes

1 EMCC International (2015) *EMCC Competences Framework V2*, September. Available at: https://www.emccglobal.org/wp-content/uploads/2018/10/EMCC-competences-framework-v2-EN.pdf (accessed 25 September 2020).
2 Ordóñez, L.D., Schweiter, M.E., Galinsky, A.D. and Bazerman, M.H. (2009) *Goals Gone Wild: The Systematic Side Effects of Over-Prescribing Goal Setting*, HBS Working Paper 09-083. Boston, MA: Harvard Business School.

9   Data gathering and analytics (31 minute read)

"Make a cup of tea" Flic had said to her voice assistant, which immediately replied with, "What's the magic word?" with no hint of sarcasm. Flic had taken a deep breath and calmly said, "please" and an emoji of a raised thumb flickered across the screen of a contraption set into the wall, morphing into a circle surrounding an attractive looking hot drink, counting down the seconds until it would be ready.

Flic had leaned against the pristine kitchen surface and stretched her legs as she brought up Rafael's data file. Graphs exploded across Flic's vision, showing his heart rate, blood pressure, and cortisol, dopamine, and serotonin levels over time. Her eyes darted around the dashboard, setting AI analytics to work and pulling in other data sources, from news feeds to social media use statistics, his calendar, and workplace information.

By the time the tea was poured, Flic had already diagnosed the situation. Rafael was clinically addicted to social media and particularly the photos of his ex-wife, who had since remarried and had a child. His working hours had become longer since entering Parliament, and he had been feeling more stressed, particularly in the immediate aftermath of having been given the office of Foreign Secretary.

Flic had taken a testing sip of the tea and made her way through to her coaching room, feeling intimidated and yet building up her courage to meet the man she felt she already knew better than she knew herself.

Know thyself

The cataclysm of 2020 led my wife to take up running, which she'd not done before. You wouldn't know it though. At one point, she was running a half-marathon every Saturday, earning her several achievements in an app on her phone. She knows how many kilometres she's run this week, her average speed and best time, how different elevations have played a part, and – most importantly – how that compares to her friends.

It turns out that runners have been doing this for a while. In 1970, Pennsylvania State University broke down athletic activities into a series of granular data points for the first time, enabling the identification of the optimised stride length, floor contact points, adaptations for gradients, and so on.[1] Fifty years on, physiological data has proliferated every area of sports. Professional athletes pore over heatmaps that reveal their movement patterns, people like my wife get insight into their running habits, and the desire for a more quantified self has grown outside of the sports arena.

Modern workplace technology now often includes statistical analyses of the amount of time spent in meetings and checking emails, and we love discovering data on ourselves. The idea that we are a quantifiable machine that we can tweak to become more effective is somehow attractive, and as much as that dehumanisation may grate with our philosophy around people, the "quantified self" philosophy and approach share core values with those of coaching. A heightened level of access to data increases self-awareness, something we strive for in our practice for our coachees.

Using data offers more advanced approaches to coaching, generating conversations that bypass many filters and biases, shining a torch onto blind spots that provide otherwise hidden opportunities for improvement.

Input options

The first sort of data we're likely to have had experience of using in coaching sessions is that of diagnostic tools that help form a basis for the coaching relationship, like CNAs, intellectual property, and simple questionnaires. Psychometrics are widely used, and while most recommend debriefs by a licensed practitioner, these can be helpful in any coaching conversations through offering a common language and framework for the coachee to apply to their understanding of themselves and those they interact with.

Psychometrics aren't perfect for several reasons, whether that's the lack of nuance, the test–retest reliability, or the science behind them. A potentially helpful alternative or complement is 360-degree feedback, offering the coachee observations and opinions from people they interact with, including peers, and those more senior and junior than them. These are becoming increasingly popular, and now form a standard part of promotion cases and even annual performance reviews in different organisations, so the output can often already be present. Given the growing standardisation of HR systems within organisations, many coachees will be able to access these sorts of information from one screen, making it an efficient way to initiate a coaching conversation, and provide a baseline for conversations to return to, particularly when a coaching platform has been configured to seamlessly interface with the performance review process.

Aside from personal performance data, it can also be relevant to draw on other data points present within the coachee's wider systems to add valuable contextual information to the coaching relationship. One example of this is data available within the coachee's organisation, such as employee engagement survey results, HR-related statistics, productivity, and audit and compliance data, as well as financial results. Having a conversation informed by one

Figure 9.1 A tailored coaching diagnostic built in Google Forms

or more of these may offer the coachee creative ways of thinking and questioning based on the hard facts as much as on experience and gut feel.

If we're feeling brave, we can also facilitate data analytics live in coaching sessions in a way that hasn't been possible until recently. A range of tools, from quantum computers for powerful analytics through to interactive data visualisation platforms (in three dimensions when in VR), are available, many accessible via a browser. For example, a coach I was supervising, Fiona, was working with a senior manager on his email communication skills. Fiona sat with the coachee as he copied and pasted the text of his ten most recent emails into a word cloud generator, which sizes the words based on how commonly they're used. She reported that the look on his face was a picture as the phrase "need this yesterday" appeared larger than any other.

Data, data everywhere

Data is now available that provides insight into almost everything we do – we all have a digital footprint. Every minute, YouTube users upload more than

Figure 9.2 A word cloud generated from worditout.com based on my most recent LinkedIn posts

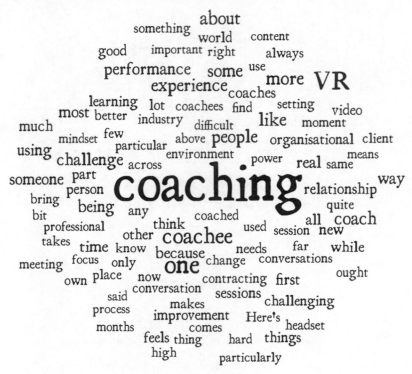

500 hours of videos, WhatsApp users send more than 40 million messages, and more than 188 million emails are sent.[2] The amount of activity and in particular communication that doesn't take place over the internet now is a tiny minority of our lives. I asked a coachee recently to break down his previous week, and it turned out he was able to answer almost exclusively using data; we discussed:

- calendar appointments
- email and instant messaging conversations
- documents he'd opened
- music and podcasts he'd listened to and at which times
- TV series he'd streamed
- internet browsing and search histories
- location timeline
- bank statements.

It turned out that not a single activity in his week hadn't been captured somewhere, which my coachee found both insightful and a bit terrifying. As we work with our coachees, drawing in this data can enrich our conversations, bringing into the light certain habits that otherwise might remain in darkness.

The Internet of Things

The first glimpse of the Apple Watch in 2015 was met with cynicism that anyone would want to pay money for a clearly overpriced product that does little more than further addict us to our phones. Roll the clock forward half a dozen years, and the Apple Watch is now outselling the whole of the Swiss watch industry.[3] Lots of people now have smart watches and smart bands, giving their owners access to information on physiological states, giving insights into exercise, sleep, and stress habits. These make it that much easier to transparently discuss goals and behaviours in coaching sessions, set deeply quantifiable goals, and track them. Several times I've had coachees state their desire to exercise more or get to sleep earlier, and this sort of data provides our conversation with a level of access to candid information we could never have had without the benefit of wearable technology (wearables).

Wearables are advancing rapidly, powered by a growing interest in the idea that technology can rapidly and reliably bridge the incommunicable gap experienced by those who throughout history have achieved self-actualisation. By recording the physiological symptoms that lie behind a state of flow or a spiritual experience, those can be reverse-engineered. Quantified self devices now include trackers for sleep, posture, heart rate variability, and sweat gland activation. It's also now possible to have kits delivered to our homes than enable insight into every data point imaginable, like cholesterol and blood glucose levels, the pH and nitric oxide levels of our saliva, DNA profiling, and even the full sequencing of our genome and microbiomes. It's possible using technology available today to have an informed conversation about a coachee's heart rate and blood oxygen levels through a smart watch or band, cortisol levels through analysing the tone of their voice,[4] skin temperature and physical movement through smart garments,[5] and even brainwaves through increasingly subtle and affordable headbands.

And the IoT is much broader than wearables, encapsulating all internet-connected devices that serve a purpose through their physical presence. The presence in one's house of a button that has been programmed to order a certain product or takeaway reveals something about what matters to them, as does a doorbell that enables a two-way conversation while on holiday, or a fridge that allows the owner to see what's inside when they're at the shops. Using data provided by this sort of product when talking to a coachee about their habits can only increase the value of a conversation based purely on their own perceptions. It's one thing a coachee saying what they're planning on eating for dinner, and quite another for them to bring up an image of the inside of their fridge.

The biggest risk associated with IoT devices returns to confidentiality. The Internet of Things could also be called the Internet of Hackable Things, and as those devices by design are connected to other devices (whether via Bluetooth to a phone or via a router to an internet service), it simply offers another entry point for a cybercriminal.

Mobile apps

Smartphones are now omnipresent, an extension of ourselves to the point that the majority of adults are almost never more than arm's reach from their phones at any time and in any location. The features that have expanded smartphones' capabilities have exponentially increased their sway over our behaviours, anticipating our movements, interrupting us throughout the day, and capturing information on every habit that involves technology, which is now almost limitless.

The power of the smartphone lies in the data it has access to, some of which is accessible to view, and that can add real gravity to a coaching conversation, as discussed above. The sorts of apps that we use on our phones give us deep insights across every behavioural axis, from physiology to the way we spend our time and our money, available within seconds. I was once working with a coachee who disclosed how aware she was of her tendency to travel using Uber when other options were available. It was costing her money she didn't want to spend, and changing her habits away from reading on the Tube and towards scrolling through her phone in the car. Both of these were contributing to a daily existence she wasn't grateful for. The coaching sessions that followed started with a review of her Uber journeys; the fact that she was going to have to show me had an effect on reducing her use, and within two months she'd uninstalled the app. When awareness and an attempt at effort don't have an effect, accountability tends to do the job.

One of the most helpful datasets afforded by smartphones, ironically, can be found in the form of digital wellbeing settings, capturing how many notifications the phone has received, how many times it's been unlocked, and how long the screen has been on among other things. Smartphones are wondrous works of technology that carry many negative side effects, among which screen addiction sits head and shoulders above the rest. Most people under-report how much they use their smartphone, and are shocked when they see the cold statistics, often revealing several hours lost each day to social media and casual gaming apps.

The data offered to us by smartphones, particularly alongside other technologies, can add weight to understanding a problem, galvanising a call to action in the coachee. And mobile apps can form part of the practical solution as well, with some designed to track, gamify, and/or nudge our behaviours in the right direction. Would it be helpful for us to curate a list of apps we favour, so that when, for example, a coachee is having trouble sleeping, we can recommend one immediately? Some of the apps on our phones have disconcertingly more control over our behaviour and underlying attitudes than self-discipline does. Wouldn't it be a great testimony – if not a little ironic – to the power of tech-savvy coaching for a coachee to take an action in a coaching session to start using a notification or app blocker that contributed to them breaking their FOMO[6]-fuelled screen addiction?

The trick here is quantifying objectives into measurable "micro goals". For example, a coachee I just finished working with who wanted to develop an attitude of constant learning set herself the goal of listening to only one minute of an informational podcast each day, tracking this among other activities in an app that rewarded her through levelling up a fantasy hero avatar. The meaningless addition of better clothing and facial features produced enough dopamine that she saw success in a way that she hadn't until that point.

Some unique risks posed by data analytics

Any time we encounter the word "data", our internal warning system should be pointing us towards the word "confidentiality". Data exists somewhere physically, whether at rest on a device somewhere or in transit – often both – and in either state it will be accessible by users other than us and our coachees. Without the right safeguards in place it will be unprotected from inappropriate access, and even with strong protection the risk never entirely disappears. In addition to that, we encounter a specific new set of risks related to data analytics that are worth increasing our awareness of.

Blind trust

Whether it's down to our anchoring bias or something else, there's something about a graph that makes facts more convincing, even when they're particularly unexpected. But datasets often give an incomplete or skewed version of the truth. For example, the digital wellbeing dashboard may confidently say that a coachee spent two hours playing games on their phone today, when in actual fact they had racked up a further three hours on a second device.

This happens all the time. It was widely publicised in April 2020 that the UK Government's figures on COVID-19 cases and deaths were understated by more than a third.[7] The reasons for this take us back to the points raised about accuracy in Chapter 4. Our attitude towards data to enable us to interrogate it properly will support our coachees to gain the best quality insights thanks to – and sometimes in spite of – the data being presented to them.

Correlation implying causation

Data analytics can be a very challenging discipline, because the principle of cause and effect is not as observable in real life as we'd like it to be. Even something as widely accepted as the fact that smoking causes lung cancer is difficult to prove at first glance because of the delays involved; it could take decades for smoking to have that effect, and so many other factors are also at play that it isn't immediately obvious that it's doing what the claims suggest.

In contrast, some data points seem to be exhibiting a cause and effect relationship when we're actually observing a coincidental correlation. Consider the fact that, in the US, the number of computer science doctorates awarded correlates with the total revenue generated by arcades, to a surprising degree. Without the axis headings, only a fool would conclude that these two series are not directly connected, and yet it's clear that this conclusion is the right one. With enough data points, the chances that two of them will have a high correlation coefficient becomes quite high, making it difficult to identify what's connected and what's not.

Unjustified extrapolation

Polling data in recent years has been revealed as imperfect, from the UK and US elections to the Brexit vote. There are multiple factors at play, from the structure of the ballot system to the skewed demographics of those who participate in polls, and one important lesson rises above the rest: the results of one population do not necessarily hold true over another. The financial services regulators are more aware than most about this, and require investment managers to undermine their boasting of consistent year-on-year growth with a phrase that communicates: "past performance is not a reliable indicator of future results".[8]

In addition to this, we face the challenge of living in a world that in many ways is far too complex to define. The number of atoms in the average human adult exceeds the total number of bytes in the entire internet by a factor of seven. Any data analytics therefore over-simplifies reality by design, which could easily lead to conclusions being made that are accurate based on the dataset in question, but which don't hold true outside of it. Take the criminal justice system in America, for example, which is facing ongoing challenges due to mass incarceration falling disproportionately on less privileged communities. The fact, however, that almost all US prosecutions happen at a local level,

Figure 9.3 Example of how correlation should not be used to imply causation

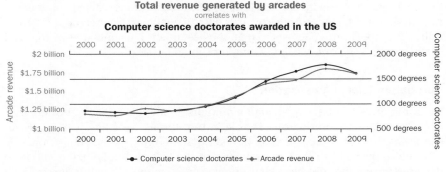

Source: Vigen, T., Total revenue generated by arcades correlates with Computer science doctorates awarded in the US. Available at: https://www.tylervigen.com/ (accessed 28 September 2020)

means that "the criminal justice system" is in effect many entities rather than one, and insights from data in one city may produce the opposite effect in another location.

Let's say that we introduce an evaluation and feedback form that generates results for all of our coachees in one database. A cursory glance over the data may suggest that, say, coachees are achieving their objectives sooner when coaching sessions happen in the morning. As rational as it may feel for us to move forward with a policy to only book sessions in the morning, it may not be justified, for two reasons:

1 It may not be true for the entire population, despite being true for the majority; every coachee is unique, and for that matter every coaching session is unique.
2 This population may not be representative of all populations; past coachees are not reliable indicators of future coachees!

Over-segmentation

One of the simplest and most powerful activities to perform in data analytics is to segment data, which helps to identify correlations and enable more conscious action. A global company I was working with recently had identified that across the employee base, men were paid more than women on average – this came as a disappointment and a surprise for them, because of the amount of work that had gone into addressing this over the previous twelve months. The truth is that the overall summary wasn't the whole picture. By segmenting the dataset by grade, it became immediately apparent that pay was essentially identical at all grades except at the most senior positions, which led to a skew in the data as they earned disproportionately more.

The problem is that segmentation in developing goals with coachees requires a level of skill and intuition, due to the inherent complexity that exists within each one of us. A prerequisite of segmentation is creating a smaller dataset, within which anomalous results will have distortive effects. As a result, while segmenting further might feel like it will provide greater insight, it may actually be misleading.

This was particularly highlighted in the immediate aftermath of the 2020 US election. Benford's Law, which observes that in many naturally occurring datasets the leading digit is disproportionately more likely to be smaller than larger, was overlaid against polling data in an attempt to prove that fraud had taken place. Informed users of Benford's Law, however, pointed out that the artificial creation of similar-sized counties would lead it to report anomalies as a matter of course.

Bias

One day while writing this chapter, *The Guardian* (a left-wing newspaper) and *The Daily Telegraph* (a right-wing newspaper) both ran the same story on their front page. One bore the headline, "Tory rebels set to fail",[9] while the other proclaimed, "Tory rebellion grows".[10] The facts within them were fundamentally the same, but their framing in the newspaper intentionally led the reader to entirely opposite conclusions. If you have a brain, you have bias, and this is no more obvious than in the world of data analytics. It's nice to think that the numbers don't lie, but in many cases the lightest questioning will lead to clear issues of bias being surfaced.

This can happen the moment the data is captured, with humans capable of subjectively misinterpreting the most carefully worded of questions more often than anyone would predict. We also bring our bias to our interpretation of data. This year, my son had his first opportunity to stand for election to join the school council. Every class in the school could have male and female representatives, and in my son's class every boy stood for election while only a handful of girls did. While sharing this story with two friends, one saw it as evidence of the patriarchy's intrusive presence at such a young age, while the other saw it as evidence of the fundamental differences between men and women. Maybe both or neither of those statements are true, but the data is no more than just that – drawing conclusions and deciding on actions will always run the risk of our own biases.

Trajectory and velocity

A lot of the power in data analytics sits in **big data**; vast, multifaceted datasets combined with the potential of AI to predict the future, which has reached absurd levels of accuracy. Machines can predict someone's ethnicity and Big Five personality traits from their Facebook likes more accurately than their friends and family can (with the exception of spouses),[11] face-detection software can predict sexuality better than humans can,[12] an algorithm has been developed that can predict someone's going to hand in their notice before they know they're going to,[13] and some companies are now able to accurately predict and automatically order stock that sells within 30 days with a 90% success rate.[14]

Every series of events, decisions, and actions has a direction of travel. The trajectory of data analytics has been to use more data in a more automated fashion and to distribute it across more parties to gain better insights. The speed of this growth, unsurprisingly, has been accelerating, and is showing no signs at all of slowing down. The other risks faced are therefore constantly expanding.

TL;DR

Data is a helpful, objective source to help increase self-awareness in our coachees, and is already used in many coaching engagements in the form of diagnostics such as psychometrics and 360-degree feedback. The amount of data we have access to at the present time is vast, in which almost all of our coachees' activities will be quantified to a certain extent, including IoT devices and activity that uses the internet. Mobile apps can be helpful for gathering this data and forming part of the solution through nudges and gamification.

Data analytics presents some specific risks alongside concerns about confidentiality, specifically:

- the trust we blindly place in the outputs of data analytics
- correlation in a dataset being incorrectly interpreted as causation
- extrapolation of correct conclusions to an unjustified wider dataset
- segmentation that unhelpfully distorts and skews conclusions
- bias in data capture, analysis, and application
- an increasing use of big data, AI, and other data-hungry predictive analytics, exacerbating every other risk.

Notes

1 Nelson, R.C. (1970) *A Study to Determine the Biomechanics of Running in Skilled Trackmen*, Final Report, Project No. 8-B-012, Washington, DC: US Department of Health, Education, and Welfare, Office of Education. Available at: https://www.wired. com/wp-content/uploads/archive/images/multimedia/magazine/1707/Nelson_Running_Speed.pdf (accessed 24 September 2020).

2 DOMO (2018) *Data Never Sleeps 6.0.* Available at: https://web-assets.domo.com/blog/ wp-content/uploads/2018/06/18-domo-data-never-sleeps-6.png (accessed 17 November 2020); DOMO (2019) *Data Never Sleeps 7.0.* Available at: https://web-assets. domo.com/blog/wp-content/uploads/2019/07/data-never-sleeps-7-896kb.jpg (accessed 17 November 2020); DOMO (2020) *Data Never Sleeps 8.0.* Available at: https://web-assets.domo.com/blog/wp-content/uploads/2020/08/20-data-never-sleeps-8-final-01-Resize.jpg (accessed 17 November 2020).

3 Strategy Analytics (2020) Apple Watch outsells the entire Swiss watch industry in 2019, *Strategy Analytics* [press release], 5 February. Available at: https://news. strategyanalytics.com/press-releases/press-release-details/2020/Strategy-Analytics-Apple-Watch-Outsells-the-Entire-Swiss-Watch-Industry-in-2019/default.aspx (accessed 28 September 2020).

4 Matheson, R. (2014) "Moneyball for business": Startup's behavioral analytics on employees uncover ways to increase workplace productivity, satisfaction, *MIT News*, 14 November. Available at: https://news.mit.edu/2014/behavioral-analytics-moneyball-for-business-1114 (accessed 9 October 2020).

5 Microsoft Technology Licensing, LLC (2016) *United States Patent Application Publication: Modular Wearable Device for Conveying Affective State*, Pub. No. US 2016/0133151 A1, 12 May. Available at: https://pdfaiw.uspto.gov/.aiw?docid=20160133151&SectionNum=1&IDKey=2D6406993DBE (accessed 9 October 2020).

6 Fear of missing out.

7 McIntyre, N. and Duncan, P. (2020) Care homes and coronavirus: Why we don't know the true UK death toll, *The Guardian*, 14 April. Available at: https://www.theguardian.com/world/2020/apr/14/care-homes-coronavirus-why-we-dont-know-true-uk-death-toll (accessed 28 September 2020).

8 Financial Conduct Authority (2018) *FCA Handbook: COBS 4.6 Past, simulated past and future performance (non-MiFID provisions)*. Available at https://www.handbook.fca.org.uk/handbook/COBS/4/6.html (accessed 29 September 2020).

9 Walker, P., Murphy, S. and Quinn, B. (2020) Tory rebels set to fail in bid to tackle virus laws, *The Guardian*, 29 September, p. 1.

10 Hope, C. (2020) Tory rebellion grows over PM's handling of the pandemic, *The Daily Telegraph*, 29 September, p. 1.

11 Youyou, W., Kosinski, M. and Stillwell, D. (2015) Computer-based personality judgments are more accurate than those made by humans, *Proceedings of the National Academy of Sciences USA*, 112 (4): 1036–1040. Available at: https://doi.org/10.1073/pnas.1418680112.

12 Kosinski, M. and Wang, Y. (2017) Deep neural networks are more accurate than humans at detecting sexual orientation from facial images, *Journal of Personality and Social Psychology*, 114 (2): 246–257.

13 Clark, J. (2014) Big data knows when you're going to quit your job before you do, *Bloomberg News*, 29 December. Available at: http://www.bloomberg.com/news/2014-12-29/big-data-knows-when-you-re-going-to-quit-your-job-before-you-do.html (accessed 25 April 2016).

14 Briggs, F. (2017) OTTO uses Blue Yonder to increase customer demand through improved delivery times, *Retail Times*, 9 March. Available at: http://www.retailtimes.co.uk/otto-uses-blue-yonder-increase-customer-demand-improved-delivery-times/ (accessed 13 November 2020).

10 Coaching conversations (42 minute read)

Rafael's hologram had emerged into the empty chair Flic had set up in her coaching room, revealing a man whose posture and facial expression presented boldness mixed with anxiety. Flic had immediately relaxed. Coaching conversations were her at her best self, and she wasted no time before putting him at ease with the help of subconscious binaural beats.

After some initial discussion around his background and personal values, it had become clear that his relationship with the Prime Minister, a particularly details-oriented lady called Comfort, was causing him concern. After some gentle probing from Flic, he made the discovery that three key underlying emotions were affecting the relationship. He was unjustifiably afraid of Comfort discovering a mistake in his work, intimidated by her relationships across Parliament, and frustrated at a lack of respect he felt from her. Flic asked if he would be open to experimenting with something, to which he agreed.

"Please will you accept the request to your lenses?" Flic had asked, activating a connection between Rafael's devices and her Challenging Conversations software.

He saw a request slide into his sight, which he accepted. Flic smiled as he started suddenly at the sight of Comfort entering the room, a stern expression on her face.

"I don't think I like this!" Rafael had exclaimed, his involuntary laughter betraying the truth. He waved his hand through the mirage to make sure he was still alone in his office, and settled back into his chair, anxiety now replaced with intrigue. From his perspective, Flic and Comfort were sitting opposite him. Flic nudged one of the controls delicately, and Rafael saw Comfort turn to stare at her, looking her up and down with a hint of disdain before turning back to look directly back at him. Another nudge, and Comfort visibly relaxed, paying attention to Flic as she leaned forward.

"Let's explore those fears and frustrations" she had said, and led Rafael through three scenarios with Comfort, in which he interacted with her to directly address his concerns, before leading a time of reflection on the assumptions he'd been holding. As the session drew to a close, Rafael had thanked Flic sincerely, and his image had dematerialised.

Suddenly, Flic was violently brought back to the present by a red filter clouding her vision, a warning message descending from above.

"Oh no …" she murmured, immediately running to the door, and stumbling into the next room.

The impact of technology

One of the most tactical and exciting avenues to explore when thinking about using technology is within the arena of coaching sessions. We're constantly on the lookout for ways to improve the quality and creativity of our coaching, and technology offers options that wouldn't exist otherwise.

Adding technology into a coaching conversation changes its nature, because different environments change the dynamics of a relationship and a conversation. That isn't necessarily good or bad in itself, but needs addressing through contracting, recontracting, or spot contracting, which can at times be as beneficial as the experience of using the technology.

In late 2019, I mentioned to a new coachee, Clara, that we had the option of using video or the phone for future sessions, and she immediately froze in terror. "No" she said, "let's meet in person. I have a bit of an irrational fear of phone calls." I suggested, empathetically and playfully, that maybe our next session should be over the phone. We still met in person, but the topic did come up in our next session, and a couple of sessions later COVID-19 forced us into using video for our coaching sessions.

Clara quickly had to get used to being reliant on technology for having every professional conversation, and the same experience was true for coaches, where many had historically expressed a strong preference for meeting in person. 2020 gave us the largest case study in history of coaching being almost exclusively delivered remotely; technology makes coaching possible when it might not be otherwise, and offers ways to augment coaching sessions.

Remote coaching

All coaching delivered remotely uses technology, leading some to refer to remote coaching as "e-coaching", although use of this word is inconsistent. It's not every coach's initial preference due to the loss of those elements that build social capital: small talk, shared food and drink, eye contact, and the energy generated by sharing silence. It's also undeniably pleasant to meet in person; 2020's experience of remote working very quickly revealed the ability for organisations to operate with a remote workforce and what a disaster for well-being it would be were society to adopt that mindset.

Remote coaching has its benefits, effectively removing the challenge of travel, eliminating the associated financial, time, and environmental costs. It also unlocks new ways for the coachee to experience the coaching session. For example, coaching while walking can be a catalyst for opening different sorts of coaching conversations as the environment shifts, and doing this remotely removes the awkward moments of needing to discuss which direction to walk in.

That said, when delivering coaching remotely, confidentiality should remain front of mind. When shut inside a physical space, we are conscious of our ability to be overheard, which may not be the case when coaching remotely. Keeping the coachee conversation private, such as through wearing headphones at all times, is of fundamental importance, and more technical concerns over unencrypted traffic are valid.

Phone

One of the most basic forms of remote coaching is to simply speak over the telephone. It can feel like a loss to have to drop visual cues, and it's certainly different from meeting in person, and yet most of us find that the lack of visual sensory information increases our ability to lean into the auditory space. When coaching over the phone, I find myself closing my eyes to truly pay attention to my coachee's tone of voice, and genuinely hearing the words they use.

The foundational work of neurolinguistic programming, Bandler and Grinder's *The Structure of Magic*,[1] uses annotated transcripts showing how a therapist is at their most effective when they do little more than asking: "What do you mean when you say such and such?" When physically present with someone, it can be difficult to have such a high level of conscious awareness of the words being used that they can be dealt with in that way. Coaching via the phone removes the distraction of the coachee's physiology and any awareness of our own physical presence, unlocking new depths in the coaching experience that would have been difficult to achieve otherwise.

Text

We email frequently, comment on social media posts, and exchange instant messages as second nature, so is it odd that there hasn't been a massive surge in text-based coaching conversations? I happen to not think so – there's a big difference between text coaching and any other form: it's much more natural being used asynchronously. It's quite possible to send a question in a text message format and not expect to receive a response for several hours depending on the coachee's availability.

That asynchronism has pros and cons. To its advantage, it's indisputably convenient. No longer does a coachee need to carve out two hours to fit into an already packed schedule when they can simply send a message and be in a coaching experience. And the time pressures for both coach and coachee simply aren't present when the interaction isn't time-bound. The coach no longer feels performance anxiety to have to formulate the perfect next question, and the coachee can genuinely take as much time as they need to answer something particularly profound. In these cases, we should encourage our coachees to record themselves speaking rather than curating a succinct text-based reply.

Its strength is its weakness. One of the primary gifts that coaching offers to coachees can be uninterrupted time to think, and when a coaching interaction becomes no more than yet another interruption to fill the coachee's already overfull time, that gift is lost. And then there's the tension introduced in a coaching session when we simply sit in silence, asking provocative and empowering questions through no more than the act of paying attention. That potency is lost when the experiences of being paid attention to and not are identical.

There's also the additional challenge of solipsistic introjection,[2] the phenomenon of a reader adding the self-created sound of the writer's voice to the words in their mind. Considering that a big value in coaching is to unravel some of the cognitive biases and filters coachees hold, having those applied to the words "spoken" by a coach feels a bit counter-intuitive.

Video

Video coaching is now widely used and offers most of us a close enough experience to that of being physically with a coachee. It's undoubtedly different though, and so it's worth reflecting on what we need to change to deliver as effective an experience as we would were we with them in person. There are some obvious benefits from video coaching: saving travel time and cost, saving office space, increasing privacy when coach and coachee are in their own homes (sometimes – interruptions tend to be higher at others), and enabling coaching to take place across international borders. In addition to those, we are empowered to be more attuned to our coachees while coaching via video. Because of the lack of ability to truly maintain eye contact, its intensity is removed, enabling us to truly pay attention without feeling pressurised to look away, while coachees feel freer to disclose. And we're far more flexible in terms of movement during video calls; a coach who can't leave the house for valid reasons could lead a session while the coachee engages in a wonder walk, which wouldn't be possible otherwise.

There is a potential issue in video coaching that lies deep in our neurology, in that the two-dimensional face that we appear to be having a conversation with is clearly not a physical human being. At a sensory level, a face on a screen is no different from a news broadcaster, and yet we are interacting with them somehow. This unconscious sense that something's not quite right can make our minds feel that the thing pretending to be a human in front of us is a threat. Encouraging the odd moment of becoming consciously present can overcome those feelings by engaging the executive cognitive functions to be reminded of the reality.

There are also heightened risks around transference and countertransference, and intuition in general, when the physical spaces inhabited by us and our coachees are different. The lack of shared visual cues combined with the multiple layers of aural interpretation happening in our minds can nudge us in directions we would never pursue were we with our coachees as an embodied presence.

Coaching through video can be liberating, as we gain travel time back, and benefit from the focus of the time to see sessions shorten, but some of the behaviours it tends to activate are unhealthy. It's tempting to fill that saved travel time with more video calls, and our sedentary state while delivering a day of coaching sessions combined with the attention needed to be present online is exhausting. Forcing ourselves to take breaks, and looking after our physical environment, including both the room and our bodies, is indescribably important. It might sound silly, but I know that I'm a better coach when I've just had a hot cup of tea and can smell the incense I hide to one side of the screen.

We ought to also make the most of the control we have over video coaching to artificially induce rapport. Being mindful about what our coachees see when we switch our cameras on will help us to craft an environment that sends the signals we want to. Depending on the coachee, positioning behind ourselves a certificate of our coaching accreditation, a photo of our children, an easel containing our latest creative exploration, a minimalistic piece of Nordic furniture, or a cared-for plant will generate different thought patterns in our coachees and unconsciously shape the experience for them.

And let's not get too attached to the idea of staring into the tiny dot in the same laptop we access our emails on, however convenient that might be. By entering a video coaching session on our smartphone, several additional benefits suddenly present themselves:

- The camera and the screen are in far greater proximity on a phone, allowing for much closer experience of eye contact for our coachees.
- Phones give us greater flexibility to move to different locations to assist with the coaching experience
- Accessing a session from two devices provides options for creative sharing of screen content while retaining engagement with the video feed of our coachees

Virtual reality

To foster a sense of embodied presence while meeting remotely, it's hard to not be tempted by VR, despite a tendency among VR professionals to have a particularly narrow and directive definition for coaching that in most cases doesn't include a coach. Professional VR devices are becoming more affordable, with Cardboard[3] enabling the creation of a low but passable quality VR headset for the price of a coffee, while more expensive options offer incomparable experiences, with options now designed specifically for the corporate market.

These give us the benefits of a distraction-free environment that encourages embodied learning through increased tendencies to gesticulate, which research has shown increases its effectiveness.[4] On top of that, we get the opportunity to meet our coachees in virtual locations such as in an inspiring meeting room, deep in a forest, high on a mountaintop, underwater, in orbit, and a whole range of fantastic spaces.

Not only are the locations inspirational in themselves, giving a coachee a very different visual experience from our face appearing on a screen, they can be easily changed midway through a session to enhance a coaching experience by activating a different set of stimuli or tapping into a metaphor, whether that's assisting in meditation through being placed on a deserted beach, hovering above a city to reflect on the systems at work, or practising a presentation on a conference stage in front of a dynamically responsive crowd. More than once I've coached people in VR locations in which the conversation has taken directions clearly inspired at least as much by our context as my coaching presence.

The technology is getting excellent in the newest headsets. Concerns about VR causing nausea have now been solved through unbelievably high resolutions and full inertial measurement units containing triple axis accelerometers, gyroscopes, and magnetometers, used in conjunction with multiple cameras and LED constellations to make the experience as immersive and comfortable as possible. Even with stylised environments and avatars, our hyperawareness of the false environment fades away remarkably quickly.

In fact, VR experiences that look like a high-quality cartoon are better in most circumstances than attempts to accurately recreate reality for two reasons. One of these is our disquiet with imperfection, which we'll revisit when looking at AI coaches. The other is the ability VR gives us to visually present ourselves however we'd like; unconscious biases play much less of a role in a fictional world in which every avatar looks similar. And this is only half of the

Figure 10.1 vTime XR, a cross-reality platform.

benefit for those for whom a disability might tend to attract bias; navigation in VR, rather than relying on the fine motor skills required for keyboard and mouse, is optimised for eye tracking and voice recognition, offering a low barrier for entry.

Concerns around social presence are as valid in VR as they are in other forms of remote coaching. On one level VR provides unique challenges due to the lack of familiarity most of us and our coachees have with the technology – the phone is still more culturally familiar than video, and VR may be a step too far for some. On another, however, the immersive experience of VR brings a closer experience to that of meeting in person than video can achieve, particularly thanks to the reintroduction of that rapport-building eye contact and haptic, multisensory feedback, even when that's with a clearly fictitious avatar.

Sitting alongside VR in the market is **augmented reality (AR)**, which overlays digital content onto the real world and can be experienced at a basic level through live translation of foreign languages in a camera, or the many selfie filters now available.[5] While in the future AR will offer opportunities for remote coaching, its uses at present are much more tangible when meeting in person, as we'll revisit below.

Coaching enhancements

One of the big questions many of us have is how we can most helpfully and appropriately introduce technology into a coaching session. And for most of us, a technology that we have access to but don't use as much as we could is screen sharing. The technologies we're about to look at could mostly be used in person or remotely through sharing a screen and providing control, and so my encouragement to all of us would be to ask how we could use screen sharing to make our video coaching more creative, and there are plenty of ideas to make this work.

Content

As a general rule, we have access to a greater wealth of articles, podcasts, and video recordings than most other people, thanks to technology. This sort of material helps bring more variety to our coaching, and offers us an improved ability to suggest content that coachees may find helpful. For example, a coachee struggling with personal productivity is perfectly capable of designing a cohesive system for themselves, and yet sharing a link to David Allen's TEDx talk on GTD[6] might provide a kickstart for a more mature conversation.

Discussing topical content can be a genuinely useful activity, increasing the value of the coaching time together, and therefore the quality of the outcomes, but it's not without its flaws. In an already busy world, most coachees struggle to take the time out to deeply focus on a motivational presentation or life-changing book. Technology provides one solution to that problem, by enabling the sharing of content in the moment. It's entirely within our control – and at times it might be our ethical duty – to take the initiative live in a coaching session, and play a video clip we think is going to positively affect our coaching conversation.

More broadly, technology offers a different lens on the coaching process, extending it beyond a series of conversations to include the conscious consumption of relevant content, whether trusted resources like articles and podcasts, or coach-produced material drawing on any of the impressive video creation and learning tools available. Explicitly including these within a coaching process gives greater control over the experience, adding particular value to coaching engagements that sit as part of leadership development programmes, and further making the case for a coaching platform that gives clarity, consistency, and greater oversight.

Another sort of content we are getting more of a choice to reflect on together is data being generated by biofeedback monitors, like the wearables we discussed in the last chapter. It can be a powerful coaching moment to ask a coachee to describe what they're feeling in their body as they describe an event they're feeling particularly anxious about, then again after taking ten deep breaths. For some coachees, it can be much more powerful to show them a recording of their pulse and blood oxygen levels.

Making a call on when to share content using technology in the moment needs us to carefully consider whether it's a good use of time, whether it will break rapport, the quality of internet connections, energy levels in the session, and so on. There's a reasonable chance that we'll make the wrong call in either direction from time to time, and that would be a valuable thing to bring to supervision. Something we can all do is to prepare a handful of our favourite images, text, audio, and video content, and save them as bookmarks to reduce the time needed to find them. This is particularly important when coaching in VR, because of the break in rapport needed if we need to remove our headset to find it on a browser. Uploading trusted content to the VR platform library beforehand provides an integrated experience for the coachee.

Collaborative documents

A coaching conversation is co-designed in an emergent fashion by us and our coachees. As such, we should be hungry for technology that encourages that co-designed process, and virtual whiteboards are helpful for this, particularly when working with teams and groups. At the entry-level end of the spectrum, only really practical in one-to-one settings, giving another individual control over a document via screen sharing is helpful, and there are slicker tools that allow for collaboration in the moment, for example:

- with some products, documents can be shared and edited by multiple users in real-time from their own devices
- simple whiteboards are often contained within video conferencing packages

- more advanced whiteboard offerings provide the option to create intricate mood and vision boards
- chat, poll, and interactive presentation functionality with group video calls can make the space more inclusive.

Particularly with the more complex elements of these, it's worth getting as familiar as possible with them before a coaching session so we can help our coachees navigate in the moment and develop strategies beforehand.

Most of us will have our physical coaching toolkit that we travel with – coaches are some of the only adults who can buy children's toys for themselves and have a business reason for doing so. Similarly, it's sensible for us to prepare for remote coaching sessions by knowing which sorts of tools we want quick access to. The more advanced collaborative whiteboard products are specifically designed to allow for sticky notes, interactivity with images and documents, and so many more features that would never be possible without technology. If the value of the coaching is going to be increased through their use, why would we limit ourselves?

Avatars

Every fantasy book worth its salt begins with a map. When I wrote a fantasy book, *Escape from Portsrood Forest*,[7] I therefore ended up with a map illustrated by someone I'd connected with online, whose profile picture was of his dog. For months, that was his face as far as I was concerned, and that didn't reduce the rapport between us. The concept of representing ourselves digitally as an avatar is very normal, and using avatars to represent people and abstract concepts can be a powerful exercise to discover truths that until that point have remained hidden.

The whiteboard tools mentioned above can achieve this, and there are others specifically designed for coaching contexts that offer an experience that

Figure 10.2 Jamboard, Google's online whiteboard tool

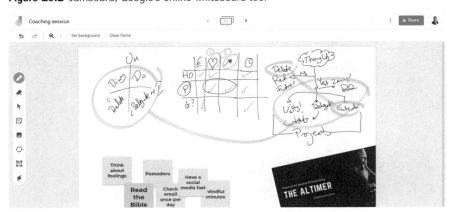

needs to be seen more than described. Some are intentionally simplistic, replicating the activity of moving physical bricks and models around a table with two-dimensional shapes. The simplicity is its power because the sense-making is being performed by the coachee.

Tools now exist that use 3D gaming technology to create a virtual space in which avatars can be placed, including shapes, symbols, and people. The coachee – and this includes full teams with multiple members simultaneously – can be in complete control, changing the perspective, sizes, stances, and movements of the various avatars to explore a metaphor of their reality, with some astonishing results. I observed a coaching session in which a coachee had created a large sphere directly in front of his avatar, which he had labelled with the name of a large project he was currently working on. Among other avatars in the scene were his children, off to one side, waving their hands frantically to get his attention. As the coachee moved the perspective – the virtual camera angle – to that of his children, there was a sudden intake of breath as he gasped, "Wow, they don't see the project at all."

Coachees will always find a way to stop the technology working the way it ought to, and our ability to maintain rapport while taking on an IT helpdesk role will only come naturally if we know where the undo button is, and which combination of menus has suddenly made the screen look the way it does. With most applications of technology in coaching, preparation is key; being a great coach isn't enough when the coachee is distracted by inexplicable error messages.

Creativity

Sometimes a coachee isn't used to describing certain topics that come up in coaching, such as personal values or emotions. When this is the case, we might

Figure 10.3 ProReal, a tool allowing users to create and explore a 3D scene using avatars

attempt to ask some questions to unlock thinking, and using some non-directive prompts, such as images on postcards, give the coachee something to explore as a metaphor to leave them with something truly memorable.

The technology isn't yet available to make this as tactile an experience as fishing through cards strewn across a floor, although to a certain extent that feels like just a matter of time. For now, there are several digital options to give similar outcomes through a variety of creative methods, such as:

- Tools that shuffle virtual decks of programmable cards for sorting concepts like personal values.
- Pleasing and provocative image cards that enable reflection and metaphor-infused discussion.
- Interactive tours of inspiring locations; many art galleries and natural wonders offer the opportunity to step into the shoes of someone there, including climbing Mount Everest, a well-used metaphor for many coaching topics.
- Creative writing devices, including story planning tools and prompts to make a narrative more tangible, and digital poetry magnets.
- Sound recording and production apps to aid in rapid reflection on a particular coachee-worded statement, or as accompaniment for improvised singing.
- Digital painting and sculpting apps to enable a coachee to reflect visually; through screen sharing, even from a smartphone, we get a better view of the work than we would if we were physically present with them, and using AR enables a coachee to physically explore a digital creation in an embodied way.

The big risk with many of these tools is that they have often been designed for uses other than coaching (such as dice and card apps designed for agile standup meeting facilitation, tabletop role-playing games, or divinations). As a result, our becoming familiar with a tool will enable us to provide appropriate direction to enhance our coachees' experience of it while remaining within our professional boundaries.

Question banks

One of the biggest challenges we face as coaches is applying a coaching model to a live coaching session for the first time. Regardless of how simple the model is, while we're trying to pay attention to the coachee, our nagging inner voice is tugging on our shirt in the background to remind us of which step comes next.

One helpful feature of video coaching, therefore, is the ability to have a coaching model up on the screen alongside the coachee's face, allowing us to give them our full attention until it's time to ask the next question. Suppressing my concern for a moment that our memories are surely affected when we have no need to remember, there are tools that have been specifically designed to

Figure 10.4 magneticpoetry.com

interweave this into the coach's experience. One text-based coaching conversation tool allows the coach to select questions from a bank specifically written for a selected coaching model. For example, the coach might select the question, "If money were no barrier, what else could you do?", editing it in the message box before clicking send.

Particularly when learning a new model, this approach is undeniably useful. We have access to the whole question bank for each coaching session, reducing the risk that we will fall into a habitual rut. That said, using this sort of technology narrows our agency in the conversation, as the effort to find the right alternative coaching model and load the relevant question bank is certainly more apparent and distracting than we would find it to shift coaching models only in our minds. Furthermore, this approach to coaching feels a touch robotic, eliminating the value brought by our humanity.

Technology for multisensory coaching

We exist in an embodied state and therefore learn most naturally when our bodies are engaged in the process rather than treated as a separate entity from our mind. As a father of four young boys, I can attest to the fact that our natural state from childhood is to engage our bodies fully in the experience of life and learning. It's therefore a helpful practice in coaching sessions to engage the fullness of our senses where possible, and the continuing rise in the practice of somatic coaching, from the Ancient Greek *soma*, meaning "body", is a testament to our recognition of this.

One tool I've found increasingly helpful as the technology has improved has been dynamically emerging soundscapes. Products are now available that generate customisable and absurdly realistic soundscapes, spanning from natural ambient sounds, to infinitely evolving music, and soundwaves that evoke alpha brain rhythms, enabling us to induce a state of wakeful rest in our coachees that is conducive to reflection and learning.

Figure 10.5 myNoise, a website hosting more than 200 dynamic sound generators

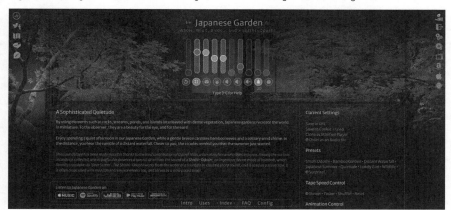

And then there's VR, a technology enabling us to be far more consciously embodied than others. VR has been demonstrated to elicit both self-reported and physiological "awe",[8] indicating that shifts in beliefs and values could be accelerated through it.[9] Some VR apps give us the ability to build shapes within the virtual space, allowing for a three-dimensional embodied exploration of a systemic representation, the ability to step out of one's avatar in a virtual version of the empty chair technique,[10] and other collaborative, creative activities in rich environments.

Additional opportunities

The introduction of technology into the coaching room expands the scope of the value that coaching can provide. The functionality to record coaching sessions, for example, is quite visible in most video platforms, offering three clear opportunities:

- for the coachee, to be reminded of the conversation and revisit what was discussed
- for the coach for personal reflection
- for the coaching supervisor or coach mentor for facilitated reflection and feedback.

An additional function that can be used with increasing levels of accuracy is transcription. Some video platforms now offer live transcription – profoundly game-changing for deaf coaches and coachees – and transcriptions of full coaching conversations are also available, whether through submitting an audio recording to a speech-to-text tool, or incorporating a live transcription service into the existing technology. This could save time and money for submitting transcripts for accreditation, and while the results can sometimes feel a bit hit-and-miss, at scale they really come into their own. An organisation with a large population of coachees could perform text analytics on the aggregate of all coaching conversations, to determine sentiment and common themes in a far more reliable way than an employee engagement survey ever could, while preserving anonymity. This could justify the investment in coaching on its own in certain circumstances, given the fact that the Financial Reporting Council has stated that traditional approaches to staff engagement are insufficient to meet the needs of the latest version of the Corporate Governance Code.

From the perspective of a coach, revisiting a session using the hard evidence rather than our perception of what happened is always a uniquely worthwhile learning opportunity, although it takes time and discipline to do it. On top of this niggling doubt that the recordings would do anything other than take up space in a folder somewhere, I'm sure I don't need to point out the confidentiality concerns that are present when recording a coaching conversation. Some coach platforms have already started to implement conversational analytics across aggregated coaching session content, meaning that the conversations all have to be held somewhere. One successful hack that reaches that sort of database will get access to an unthinkable amount of sensitive information.

TL;DR

Technology can assist directly in coaching conversations, enhancing their quality and augmenting their impact. This includes enabling remote coaching, through:

- *phone* – removing visual cues and replacing them with an increased focus on a coachee's words and tone of voice
- *text* – enabling asynchronous coaching for convenience while losing some of coaching's potency
- *video* – adding a visual element and introducing screen sharing possibilities
- *VR* – extending the embodied experience and opening up new opportunities.

It also includes technology that adds unique angles to a coaching conversation, such as:

- the ability to find and share content, including live in coaching sessions, broadening a coaching engagement to include more than just the sessions
- collaboration on interactive documents, virtual whiteboards, and chat and poll tools
- use of digital avatars to visually represent the coachee and key elements in the systems they interact with

- digital creative tools to facilitate explorative conversations for which the coachee doesn't have an existing vocabulary
- question banks to assist us in text coaching and when learning new coaching models
- technology for somatic coaching, including soundscapes and VR.

There is also the possibility to record coaching conversations in audio and transcribed formats for future reference, which presents opportunities for added value as well as raising concerns around confidentiality.

Notes

1 Bandler, R. and Grinder, J. (1975) *The Structure of Magic*, 2 volumes, Palo Alto, CA: Science and Behavior Books.
2 Suler, J. (2004) The online disinhibition effect, *CyberPsychology and Behavior*, 7 (3): 321–326.
3 A VR headset design using a smartphone championed by Google, often literally made out of cardboard.
4 Novack, M. and Goldin-Meadow, S. (2015) Learning from gesture: How our hands change our minds, *Educational Psychology Review*, 27 (3): 405–412.
5 A potential distinction can be drawn between AR and mixed reality (MR). In pure AR, the live image from a camera simply has digital content placed on top of it, while MR understands the world it is seeing in a more advanced way and can manipulate it, for example through placing an animated animal within a room, which can then hide behind furniture.
6 Allen, D. (2012) The Art of Stress-Free Productivity [video]. Available at: https://www.youtube.com/watch?v=CHxhjDPKfbY.
7 Isaacson, S. (2020) *Escape from Portsrood Forest*, independently published.
8 Defined as a self-transcendent emotion with two core features, "perceived vastness" and "a need for accommodation".
9 Quesnel, D. and Riecke, B.E. (2018) Are you awed yet? How virtual reality gives us awe and goose bumps, *Frontiers in Psychology*, 9: 2158. Available at: https://doi.org/10.3389/fpsyg.2018.02158.
10 Pugh, M., Bell, T. and Dixon, A. (2020) Delivering tele-chairwork: A qualitative survey of expert therapists, *Psychotherapy Research*. Available at: https://doi.org/10.1080/10503307.2020.1854486.

11 Robot coaches (37 minute read)

Flic dashed across the room, collapsing into an armchair. As soon as her body made contact with it, its right armrest took on a pulsating green luminescence, the word CHARGING repeatedly revealing itself.

She let out a sigh of relief as the warning indicator on her heads-up display disappeared. Her extensive smart implants and neural augmentations had only run out of battery once before, but the loss of memory and understanding had been like losing the ability to walk all over again. At first, the accident had seemed like it would end her life, but instead it had offered her the opportunity for a vastly improved one. A better immune system, improved balance, and greater cognitive functions came with only one downside: a need to recharge her bionics regularly.

Flic passed the time by bringing up the latest news, barely reading each article before moving to the next in search of something gripping enough to hold her attention. After her batteries reached the minimum amount, a dialogue box appeared in her vision:

SYNC COACHING NOTES?

Flic stabbed at the "Yes to all" option with her eyes, muttering under her breath about how something so helpful could be equally as annoying, and kept on scrolling.

At that moment, on the other side of the world, a piece of code that had been endlessly analysing an incomprehensible data stream did the robotic equivalent of clapping its hands in jubilation, beginning a sequence of actions to initiate the apocalypse.

Artificial consciousness

Congratulations! We've collectively shown real self-control to reach this point of a book about coachtech without being distracted too early by the world of AI replacing coaches altogether. It's difficult to resist the promise of such exciting and chilling predictive ponderings when the alternative is so comparatively mundane.

Science fiction stories that feature AI tend to pivot around machines gaining consciousness and/or attacking humanity. The concerns about AI coaches don't leap to this point, however, because they stem from a far more tactical terror: What use is a human coach if an AI coach is cheaper?

AI is a bit of a catch-all term relating to several different strands of technological development, at the root of which is the idea of replacing more than just human behaviour but the thinking behind it as well. In its simplest form this dons the title robotic process automation (RPA) and simply performs a series of programmed tasks based on the criteria that have been plumbed into it. In truth, this is barely any more complex than the sorts of macros any informed user can create in Microsoft Word; whenever you accidentally type "freind" and it corrects it to "friend", that's simple RPA in action. Of course, this isn't as effective or resilient as it needs to be to truly reflect human thought. I just intentionally misspelled "friend", and the system still refuses to believe that I meant to do it, the angry red squiggle a constant reminder that my text doesn't fit into its deep structure of reality. More advanced AI, known specifically as **machine learning (ML)**, would be able to cope with this, and some applications of ML are able to work with much more ambiguity.

When AI meets coaching

AI's effectiveness is judged by it beating different forms of "The Turing Test", in which a human is convinced that they are having a conversation with a person. This is critically important for coaching, which at its heart is certainly no less than a conversation. It's a fascinating concept to contemplate because coaching is such a human profession, inasmuch as we need to engage both brain hemispheres at all times, as we do in general conversations. The left hemisphere, responsible for linear thinking, sequencing, logic, and words, is relied upon for following coaching processes and the content of the conversation, and is relatively straightforward for RPA to replicate in theory. The right half, responsible for abstract thinking, creativity, intuition, context, and tone, is relied upon for coaching experimentation and challenge, and is very difficult even for the most advanced ML to replicate without narrowly defined criteria.

It's tempting to imagine machines as being faster and better than us, and yet the things that we do most naturally are the very things that we find the hardest to get machines to do. AI is exceptionally brilliant at predictable, repeatable activities such as online shopping. The convenience of buying products online is scarily efficient thanks to RPA in action, and with predictive analytics emerging powered by big data, robots now being introduced to many retail warehouses, and drones being trialled for deliveries, it's only a matter of time before we find our houses continually stocked with everything we need at all times, without a person being involved at all.

Given that machines are good at following defined processes to the letter (when humans aren't), and not so good at creative exercises and applying abstract concepts to variable circumstances, the future of AI coaching comes down in the short term to one very concerning question: Could coaching be reinterpreted in such a way that it would require no "right brain" thinking at all?

Taking a moment for self-reflection, might we ask ourselves which brain hemisphere more accurately describes our approach to coaching? Do we perform predictable, repeatable processes with unambiguous quality criteria, or is the majority of what we do a uniquely human craft, filled with abstractions, creativity, and unpredictability? As we encountered when looking at the history of coachtech, coaching is a deeply human activity at its core, and so we might conclude that AI has a bit of a mountain to climb, and yet there are some coaching approaches and models that are certainly repeatable, and in many cases very predictable.

I wonder if we could play a little game. Imagine for a moment that you are a coachee, and that I'm asking you each of the following questions in order, pausing after each one to give you space to think and speak until you feel you've fully answered each one in turn:

- "What would you like to achieve from our time together today?"
- "And how will you know when you've achieved that?"
- "OK, thank you. So, when you achieve that, what will the effect be?"
- "And how does that compare to what's happening at the moment?"
- "What else would you like to say about that?"
- "So, from everything you've just said, or anything else that now comes to mind, what is the single most important difference between your current state and your desired future state?"
- "And what would be some ways you could take action to address that difference today?"
- "What else could you do?"
- "We only have a few minutes left together, so let's write down some actions. What are you going to do before we next meet?"

That series of questions, based unashamedly on the GROW model, could fit into a lot of coaching sessions without any editing on the part of the coach. I find it slightly troubling how at first glance it's so straightforward for coaching to add value to people – it feels like it should be harder! But as we saw earlier on, the power in coaching comes down to some truly simple yet breathtakingly formidable principles. A computer programmer with the most basic working knowledge of the simplest programming language would be able to automate that series of questions in about twenty minutes. They could even market it as AI if they wanted to.

With the help of a visually pleasing GUI, this could offer a basic level of coaching to anyone with access to a computer, and if they are willing to be coached – that's always a requirement under any circumstance – they will get value from the interaction. In fact, I think back to the first coaching sessions I led while doing my initial qualification, and don't mind admitting that my coachees would probably have gotten more value out of these generic questions than the nonsense I found myself concocting.

If it's the case that this essentially free AI tool could add just as much benefit as a human coach would, with the guarantees that it would never get distracted or tired, would remain patient throughout, and would have endless capacity to coach as many people as wanted it at any time of the day or night, how on earth could one argue that an unpredictable and probably expensive human is a better option?

In fact – and probably more interestingly – how is it that all of us haven't been automated out of delivering coaching already?

Machine capability

Maybe we human coaches have maintained our monopoly on the profession because no-one's been brave enough to try automating it as simply as that. Maybe there's something going on behind the scenes in our coaching interactions that machines simply can't replicate, or at the very least there's an assumption that's the case? If that is the reason – and it isn't at all obvious that it is – the amount of time we'll have to wait until it stops being a reason at all is shortening all the time. In 2017, Oxford University published some research claiming that there's a 50% chance that AI will outperform humans in all tasks by 2060.[1]

Before moving on, just re-read that last sentence. "All tasks" is terrifyingly inclusive; that's everything from mathematical equations, which machines already outperform humans in, language translation and driving vehicles, which machines can currently do about as well as humans in certain circumstances, all the way through to things like delivering a TED talk and writing a chart-topping screenplay, which are currently difficult to imagine.

Wherever coaching sits in that spectrum, it isn't hard to envisage the experience of being coached by a robot. In my kitchen I have a voice assistant, which is capable of doing far more than I use it for, and the illusion of a conversation is mostly quite a pleasant experience. It certainly appears to be very knowledgeable, and it's more patient with my children's incessant questions about the date and the weather than any human would be. On top of that, the voice used by the device sounds more natural than robotic. Even knowing it's a machine, I'd find it difficult to argue that plugging the process we described above into it would be a significantly worse experience than receiving the GROW model delivered via a phone.

There has also been a step up in terms of tools that would probably describe themselves using the term "AI coach". All appear far more engineered than my simple process, and it isn't clear that any offer a better experience for a coachee, despite the modern Material Design feel. In spite of all of this, the world's first AI coach was actually created sixty years ago.

Joseph Wiezenbaum, a German American computer scientist, published ELIZA in 1966. ELIZA is a relatively simple computer program, versions of which can now be accessed online quite easily, which simply asks non-directive questions, in part by picking out keywords based on linguistic context. When testing it, Wiezenbaum's secretary reportedly asked him to leave the room because of how personal the conversation with ELIZA had become.

It's definitely more therapy than coaching, but that doesn't stop it being a truly helpful tool. One happy June day, I received the worst phone call I've ever experienced; a member of my family had ended their own life. Death is hard under any circumstances, and suicide is indescribably difficult to process. As I urgently made my way home, never having thought through what I'd do in that situation, I felt numb, and pulled ELIZA up on my phone. When I arrived back home to join in with the grieving, I was able to do so having properly processed my initial reaction. Without ELIZA I'd have done that far less well.

A different sort of NLP

Mobile apps are becoming more and more intuitive, minimising the amount of time required in training for new users of a system. In contrast, ELIZA is an early example of **natural language processing (NLP)**, which throws that design process away. The user simply gives an instruction using words they understand, and the program interprets those words and applies them. As AI coach developers attempt to enable free-flowing conversations, this technology is of fundamental importance, and it's improving all the time.

NLP is broadly judged to be effective based on the GLUE (General Language Understanding Evaluation) benchmark, comprising judgements on the following nine areas:[2]

- Whether a sentence is grammatically correct
- Whether a sentence has positive or negative sentiment
- Whether two sentences mean the same thing
- Whether two questions mean the same thing
- How similar two sentences are on a scale of 1–5
- Whether two sentences agree with one another, contradict, or neither (this forms two tasks, one based on news and Wikipedia content, and another based on a crowd-sourced dataset)
- Whether a sentence answers a given question
- Which word in a sentence without a pronoun is referred to by a second sentence containing one.

A GLUE league table is maintained, with a human benchmark included to show how close computers are to understanding natural language as well as humans can.[3] Or, that was the original intention. On the day I'm writing this, the human benchmark is currently sitting proudly in fourteenth place.

Thirteen NLP systems are better at human language than humans are.

Of course, that doesn't include a test for how natural it is to have a conversation with the machine, but that's just a matter of time. Google Duplex was initially launched in May 2018, and it's worth watching the video of Sundar Pichai demonstrating it.[4] In the showcase, it has a conversation that sounds so convincingly human that the crowd can't stop themselves gasping and cheering. The machine pauses to think – entirely unnecessarily other than to make the other person feel more comfortable – and interjects with the odd "um" and "mm-hmm" to give a bewilderingly convincing illusion of human interaction. If trained to deliver coaching over the phone using a simple coaching model, this would do it at least as well as a human coach would. The technology is there and capable, it simply hasn't been switched on yet.

The natural human advantage

It would appear that the only thing stopping Google, or any of the other thirteen NLP technologies that beat humans in the GLUE benchmark, from replacing all human coaches with machines is the fact that there's something in us that wants a human face attached to a coach. And even that's not so far away.

Computer graphics are so advanced now that it's becoming difficult to identify what's real and what's not. We are frequently convinced by computer-generated scenes in movies, and TV series filmed entirely surrounded by LED screens are indistinguishable from reality. Deepfake videos of celebrities saying things they never did are surfacing all the time, and the Virtual Human Toolkit from the University of Southern California Institute for Creative Technologies is achieving fascinating outcomes from dynamically generated avatars based on scientific analyses of physiology, interactive narrative, and emotions.[5] And for something that spontaneously acts without any human direction, it's worth visiting thispersondoesnotexist.com to see instantaneously generated photographs of entirely imaginary people's faces.

And then there's humanoid robots designed to look lifelike, of which there are several now. The subtle facial expressions some can now generate are hauntingly human, such as in one, "Sophia", which is officially a citizen of Saudi Arabia.[6] There's something quite eery about watching a conversation with Sophia, revealing an undeniably human trait known as the "Uncanny Valley", a term coined by Masahiro Mori, a Japanese robotics expert, in 1970.[7] He pointed out that the sense of familiarity humans feel with creatures and objects grows the more they look like a human, until they get too close to looking like one, in which case we feel very uncomfortable indeed. For example, a dog might appear cute specifically because its face looks like it has human expressions, but if we put a human face on the dog it would become disturbing. When computer graphics or humanoid robots begin to look almost, but not entirely, like a human, we really don't like it.

If coaching can only be at its best when a human-to-human relationship is present between us and our coachees, machines will never reach the quality we can offer by design, despite their enhanced abilities to stick unerringly to a particular model and use language well.

The current reality

Taking into account everything we've looked at so far, it's not surprising that there are plenty of products out there that claim to be AI coaches. Each takes a slightly different tack in its interpretation of what good AI coaching would look like, and all of them suffer from the same problems. This is captured neatly by the overuse of the term "chatbot", a word that suggests it might offer the possibility of an informal conversation, and yet which captures most often a slightly more pleasant than usual search function for a curated data table. Rather than ML-powered, NLP-based, free-flowing conversation, in which the AI coach listens attentively and asks a powerful non-directive question, the existing AI coaches act like a conversational veneer on a standardised, engineered process flow. The AI coach developers, it would appear, play to the strengths of the technology before trying to recreate the power of coaching.

The experience as a coachee, therefore, is much more heavy-handed than the coaching our profession tends to favour, as the AI coach insists on taking its coachee through a series of programmed hints and instructions. Every demonstration I've experienced of one of these tools has included a conversation like this one:

AI coach: How anxious are you feeling at the moment?
Me: Not at all right now, I'd like to think through the next year, please.
AI coach: So how intense would you say your anxiety is at the moment on a
             scale of 1–10, where 1 is not at all anxious and 10 is overwhelmed
             by anxiety?
Me: 1 right now, I'd like to think about the next year, please.
AI coach: That's great news! Just take a deep breath and appreciate the
             present moment.

Maybe I was being unfair to the tool by trying to take the conversation in a direction it didn't want to go, but how often does a coachee do that to us? Every single session? Fundamentally, I haven't felt listened to by any tool I've tried, which is a problem in a profession that considers good listening to be one of its few pillars. Worse than that, the questions felt directive and judgemental. Is it even right to call these coaches, or are they something else? It's clear that the purpose of the experience above was to assist with anxiety, and it's good to have areas of specialism, but even within those boundaries, it's really important that we, and AI coaches, coach the person not the problem. As much as it pains me to say it, the coachee in a coaching relationship doesn't have a responsibility to be fair to the coach! In short, the AI coach in this interaction simply didn't follow good coaching practice.

There's probably a simple reason for that: tools that call themselves AI coaches are really AI therapists, an area of work that has some astounding examples of good practice. One AI therapist detects sixty non-verbal cues every second, such as eye focus, body movement and stance, tone and speed of voice, and micro-expressions, to match physical energy and "intuitively" decide when to press deeper into one topic or to change it. Results have been impressive so far with soldiers suffering from post-traumatic stress disorder, with the ability to read subconscious physical cues beating many professional psychologists. The building blocks are there and operational, but it isn't coaching.

The ethics of using robot coaches

With this in mind, efforts have been made to capture hypotheses to aid the development of helpful AI coaches, such as the tactical Designing AI Coach (DAIC) framework, which states AI coaches should:

- focus on a stated outcome and have a base of validated theoretical models that support it
- have an interaction model based on the characteristics of a strong coach–coachee relationship
- be bounded by an acceptable ethical code
- understand the systemic context.

The Google Duplex tool is so convincingly human that some argued its intentional use of sounds and quirks in tonality are deceptive, misleading someone into thinking they're speaking to a human. Google has introduced an opt out at the beginning of a phone conversation after informing the recipient that they are speaking to a machine, one of the detailed aspects of transparency identified in the DAIC framework as building a strong coach–coachee relationship, and this is just the tip of the iceberg as far as questions of ethics are concerned when it comes to AI coaching.

A table reservation made by a machine will wait in a queue for as long as necessary without becoming irritable, and saves time for the customer – even taking into account the perceived deception, on the surface no harm is being done. But AI is deeper than we realise.

The reason that ELIZA works is that the questions it asks are so broad that it always feels relevant regardless of what input it's received. But really good coaching is much more than simply sitting quietly until there's a pause and then asking what the coachee would like to say next, however helpful that can be at times. More advanced coaching AI therefore needs to take that to a more focused degree, asking specific questions that one of us would, based on our having listened deeply to the coachee and following our intuition. And so we return to the fact that the AI tools need to do what's hard for machines to do: take the abstract concepts of coaching and apply them in the unpredictable setting of a specific coaching session.

Neural networks are a complex web of algorithms designed around the way the human brain operates, which spot unstated connections lying underneath a surface level of information, and are fundamental to ML. Rather than a computer programmer identifying every possible scenario and creating a long series of "if … then … else …" statements, ML learns from being fed examples of the correct behaviour, predicting some appropriate behaviour in different circumstances, and having that validated. In more advanced creative ML systems, such as thispersondoesnotexist.com, a validation mechanism based on validated good outcomes is built into the process. Instead of the machine being programmed, it's being trained. That's what's happening when we try to log onto a website and reCaptcha asks us to click every square containing a car; we're training the Google Waymo machine that will drive an autonomous car, which has already made a prediction of what the right answers are. Seeing this in action can only lead us to the conclusion that ML is capable of far more than most of us give it credit for, with image recognition and creative activities (within narrow bounds) now better than many human efforts.

ML draws on all relevant data to draw conclusions, which will inherently lead to bias. For example, data from criminal justice systems reveal that the skin colour of someone who has committed a crime correlates to the length of sentence they receive. By learning from this dataset, a machine might actively use skin colour to help make its decisions around sentence length, when it shouldn't, morally speaking. This isn't unexpected; datasets are inherently biased whether through conscious or unconscious human intervention or not. Safety datasets used to design cars favour men over women, step counters consistently underestimate the activity of homemakers, facial recognition is more accurate for those with lighter skin, and resumé screening software penalises CVs that include the word "women".[8]

The big risk in coaching AI, therefore, is not in whether the technology is capable of doing it. It already is. It's in whether the direction it takes a coaching session is as good as, or better than, a human would do, and AI faces some big challenges as far as that's concerned. The greater quantity and diversity of data used to train, the better quality the outcome, so where will this large amount of training data come from? The only truly valid population would be live coaching sessions, which would require a huge number of coachees to give their permission. And it would hardly give a diverse picture; the coaching industry is dominated by middle-class white women over the age of forty.[9]

This is an ethical question: how should a coaching AI training dataset be biased? To include a diversity of active coaches, or some other metric? And if the latter, in which ways? If a young black man with a working-class background is offered AI coaching by his employer, how will the tool produce the best outcome for him? Should it only have been trained by coaches who share his background? This is wider than simply ticking the Equality Act's protected characteristic boxes; coaches are hugely diverse in approaches and opinions. How many seconds of expectant silence should it leave, when some coaches would simply say, "as many as the coachee needs", while others would encourage interrupting?

These are not rhetorical questions; someone, somewhere is going to make that decision, and who that ought to be and what conclusion they ought to draw isn't clear. Given the makeup of the coaching population and the size of datasets needed, the debate will not be an easy one to conclude. Worse, the decision might be made unconsciously through the actions of those involved, and as intelligent and skilled as ML specialists are, they're not coaches. Worse still, some ideology may lead AI coaches to submit fully to the preferences of the coachee, replicating the horrific work of polarisation that social media has been achieving. Where the quality and impact of coaching is defined in large part by the unique experience each coach is able to offer their coachees, the promise of an AI coach who will select "the best" approach is a long way off yet.

There are still three options of bypassing that particular concern to use AI in an effective and ethical way. Firstly, an AI coach could be introduced as an initial triage in the coaching process, lightly exploring a discussion that enables those coachees needing performance coaching to get value at a low cost, with built-in escalation criteria that trigger a human coach to take over.

Secondly, AI could be brought into our coaching sessions to observe our behaviour live and act as a pseudo supervisor, either offering a chance to reflect immediately afterwards or making suggestions in the moment based on standards we want to be reminded of. A subtle prompt appearing on the screen that asks if we are becoming too directive or suggests the conversation needs more challenge could improve our effectiveness. This sort of approach is already being used in the world of sales, in which tools record and automatically summarise sales calls, and interface directly with the CRM system to identify what behaviours are having the most positive impact.

Finally, and more idealistically, might be the "digital twin", in which a robot intentionally learns from only one specific coach. In this way, a digital copy of a seriously effective coach limited in their potential only by capacity would bring them to more coachees than they could ever manage by themselves. That does feel quite dystopian, but is a valid option that at least increases transparency over the training dataset.

TL;DR

AI has evolved to a point now where predictable, repeatable, linear processes can be automated in a relatively straightforward manner, and creative processes are becoming more possible within certain constraints. Coaching is a complex combination of these, and the elements of coaching that follow more structured approaches are capable of being automated today. Where they are, they would outperform human coaches in measurable outputs, and yet coachees have a preference for working with a human for deeper reasons.

Products that claim to be AI coaches enact a narrow line of questioning that doesn't follow good coaching practice. The ethical concerns only begin there, as ML requires large training datasets in order to learn the right behaviour and the potential for appropriate diversity is limited.

More likely and more ethical applications of AI in coaching would be to:

- act as a triage and first-line performance coach, escalating to humans only where necessary
- assist and enhance a human coach's practice through observation of coaching sessions
- act as a "digital twin", reproducing one coach as an AI tool.

Notes

1   Grace, K., Salvatier, J., Dafoe, A., Zhang, B. and Evans, O. (2017) *When will AI exceed human performance? Evidence from AI experts*. Available at: https://arxiv.org/pdf/1705.08807.pdf (accessed 3 December 2020).

2   Wang, A., Singh, A., Michael, J., Hill, F., Levy, O. and Bowman, S.R. (2019) GLUE: A multi-task benchmark and analysis platform for natural language understanding, Paper presented at the *7th International Conference on Learning Representations, ICLR 2019*, New Orleans, LA, 6–9 May. Available at: https://openreview.net/pdf?id=r-J4km2R5t7 (accessed 23 September 2020).

3   https://gluebenchmark.com/leaderboard, 23 September 2020.

4   https://youtu.be/ogfYd705cRs?t=2100, 23 September 2020.

5   For more information, see https://vhtoolkit.ict.usc.edu/index.html.

6   The irony of a machine being given citizenship a year before women were allowed to drive was not lost on Sophia's creator David Hanson, who has stated his agenda for Sophia was championing women's rights.

7   Mori, M. (1970) The uncanny valley, *Energy*, 7 (4): 33–35.

8   Perez, C.C. (2019) *Invisible Women: Exposing Data Bias in a World Designed for Men*, London: Chatto & Windus.

9   International Coaching Federation (2020) *Global Coaching Study*. Available at: https://coachingfederation.org/research/global-coaching-study (accessed 18 November 2020).

Part **3**

The Future

12 A bleak future (15 minute read)

Weeks later, Rafael found himself led by his calendar into a series of meetings with foreign powers that his virtual assistant had somehow managed to schedule in such a way that even his travel time was being spent in intense debate. While his counterpart from Germany was speaking in one discussion, he made a mental note to block out breathing space in his calendar, which his assistant automatically added to his actions list.

A gap for lunch emerged at 12:30pm, and Rafael devoured the sandwich that was presented to him as he marched into his office. At 12:43pm, his world collapsed.

The lights in the room suddenly dimmed as if sunglasses had been placed on his eyes, and a notification window took up his vision:

IMMINENT NUCLEAR ATTACK PREDICTED: 95% LIKELIHOOD

Rafael's emotions leapt from confusion to horror instantaneously, and then he consciously stood to follow the processes they had talked through so many times.

"Enact Code Leona" he said, in an unfamiliar wavering voice. While the doors locked, communications channels opened, and his heads-up display transformed the large table in front of him into a command operations centre shared with the other key players. He cleared his throat and took a deep breath.

Competing interests

We've spent the last several chapters talking almost exclusively about the interactions between coaches and coachees, which is perfectly natural and to be expected. The majority of coaching activity takes place between these two parties, and yet the decisions over which coachtech to use and how to implement it will be made by different stakeholders. Far greater influence will be held by coaching sponsors, whose hands are often tied by organisational policies, budget restrictions, and political agendas, and the technology companies that are driven at least as much to increase use of the tools (that is, addiction) as to increase their effectiveness.

The unfortunate truth for us is that it won't be enough for the coaches of the future to simply be good coaches. Technology will have a tendency to increase efficiency that we won't be able to match if we don't have access to it. Those of us who find ourselves with an instinctive aversion to technology will reach a point of having to hang up our coaching shoes sooner than any of us could predict, so it will be important for us all to start to build those skills as soon as possible. And even for those of us who have a natural affinity for technology and for whom many of the recent coaching innovations feel exciting and a way to enhance our coaching practice, there's a real risk that demand for human coaches in any form will dry up, in the same way as the introduction of the motor car saw horse populations decline drastically. Modern technology is now making coaching available at greater scale, at a lower price point, and with less of a need for people to be involved than ever before.

If this feels alarmist, let's embrace that sense of fear for a moment – working with emotions we consider bad is a healthy thing to do. This chapter by design is going to feel negative, and it's important to notice that the coaching profession is only just starting to experience a disruptive shift that has been happening elsewhere. It has been predicted that 800 million people will lose their jobs to automation by 2030, which works out to almost one in three of all workers globally.[1] That headline number shouldn't be misinterpreted – under some scenarios all of those displaced workers could retrain into different jobs, given sufficient IQ and inclination – but it would fundamentally shake the coaching profession into becoming something significantly different from its form today, to the point that the word "profession" might not be relevant any more if no-one *professes* to be practising it.

Whether it's self-service checkouts changing the role of the checkout assistant into an exceptions-driven customer service and technical support role, or the rise of autonomous electric vehicles removing the need for professional drivers and workers in the engine supply chain, it's not hard to understand the consumer attitude and behaviour that's driven by getting a more efficient outcome. One of the big challenges for our profession that therefore needs consideration is the thought that demand for us as coaches may evaporate altogether over the next 10–15 years.

Aggregated risks

We've already spent plenty of time throughout this book thinking about the benefits of particular pieces of technology and their associated risks. Those are important to think about one at a time, and yet none of the technologies we've talked about will be used in isolation. At a simple level, any given coaching engagement will use multiple pieces of technology throughout its lifecycle, both inside and outside of the coaching sessions. And at a more complex level, the various products and services will interact with one another, sharing data, and enhancing the functionality of the entire coaching experience. The same, therefore, is true of the risk profile, which can only compound with each additional component added into the overall picture. From this perspective, using several pieces of technology that by themselves might present a very low risk might result in a higher risk when assessed at a more holistic level. This means that the risks we all run with any given coachee are probably higher than we realise.

And this isn't even the biggest concern. The impact of a risk crystallising within a specific coaching relationship, while potentially devastating for the coachee, will probably be overcome in time, and will have only limited ramifications for the rest of our practice. We'll learn, make some changes, and move on. But as our risks combine with one another's thanks to the scalability of technology, the macro-level risks run by our profession as a whole become increasingly noticeable. It doesn't take an overactive imagination to conjure up a future in which coaching platforms are subsumed into one another, with an acquisition from a big player ending up dominating the industry, and when that's the case what happens if that single platform's security flaw is taken advantage of?

Imagine if the confidential coaching conversations of half the world's coachees were suddenly exposed to public scrutiny. What effect would that have on the openness of coachees across every coaching conversation? The impact of the damaging information that would come out of a data breach like that is unthinkable on the personal and professional lives of the affected coachees. And more than that, the importance of trust in a coaching relationship, enabled so clearly by its confidential nature, could be undone, hampering the value that coaching engagements in general would be able to demonstrate.

Unfortunately, this sort of event is surely only a matter of time. The data breaches that have hit the headlines historically have generally been the loss of credit card details, which is bad but in the grand scheme of things more a momentous inconvenience than an earth-shattering catastrophe. In contrast, think about the effect of the 2014 iCloud photos leak, which has undermined trust in the security of iCloud, despite it almost certainly having taken place due to individuals sharing passwords rather than a security flaw, and has caused great harm to the individuals whose private photos have now been distributed widely across the internet and will not disappear.

If we get to a point as a profession in which we're incapable of operating without technology, we will have lost the heart of coaching as a practice, and that dependence will come back to bite us. As Francis Bacon said about money, technology is a great servant but a bad master. It's therefore imperative that we, and the rest of the coaching ecosystem as a whole, from coaching supervisors and professional bodies to coaching sponsors and the technology providers themselves, make sure that our exit strategy is drawn up even as we're entering into using more technology.

Coaching foundations

In the previous chapter we explored some of the issues facing the development of AI in the coaching space, so let's allow this to proceed to its natural conclusion. The last several decades have seen a huge amount of effort poured into professionalising the coaching industry, and more effort still is needed to bring the sort of consistent quality and approach that most buyers of coaching would like to see. Technology, while offering an immediate solution to consistency across the board, moves the centre of gravity – at least as far as codes of ethics and competency frameworks are concerned – away from the professional bodies, and even away from us as coaches, towards the technology companies that control the underlying data and algorithms, most of which will have been written by people who aren't coaches and may not even understand what professional coaching is.

If the hands that are coding the tools used within the coaching industry belong to heads that haven't bought into a definition of coaching that we collectively agree on, they will be working on a set of unstated assumptions that are almost certainly going to be wrong. We laid aside an entire chapter in the initial stages of this book to state that coaching is a conversation-led change tool that is confidential, non-directive, non-judgemental, and challenging. If the bright minds that craft the coachtech of the future think of coaching as a personal motivation tool to give advice based on a biased definition of good examples, with a sub-purpose of increasing addiction to the technology and its related products, the whole of the coaching profession as we know it will collapse, and no-one will realise until it's too late.

This raises the important question, for which the answer isn't as obvious as we might think: Is that a bad thing? On the surface, of course it is – we don't want our hard work to be undone – but that misses the point, because when it comes down to it, coaching isn't about us. The purpose of our profession is to catalyse positive change in coachees and the systems in which they operate. When it boils down to it, coaching is simply kindness in action; as Paul of Tarsus so eloquently put it: "If I have prophetic powers, understanding all mysteries and knowledge, and all faith, so as to remove mountains, but have not love, I am nothing."[2] If a slight semantic tweak in our collective understanding of what coaching is will guarantee an increase in its effectiveness at achieving that purpose in all circumstances, without negating it through an increased level of risk, we should welcome it, however humbling a process that might be.

And yet, my hunch remains that we should retain a high level of scepticism about any disruptive change forced upon us by technology. If something other than coaching will catalyse more change, then we should be supportive of that, just as we would if we were to encounter a situation with a coachee that prompted a different sort of intervention, such as therapy or training. But if we end up as passengers on a vehicle driven by technology that is taking us to a very different destination from the one we collectively agreed to reach, the future of our profession is looking bleak.

TL;DR

The future of the coaching profession is going to include, and be influenced by, technology. While we may have some influence over that, most decisions around that trajectory will be made by coaching sponsors and technology providers, and barely at all by coachees.

The risks presented by the introduction of a piece of technology need to be considered at an aggregate level, in terms of their cumulative effect on a coaching relationship's risk profile and that of our whole profession. An incident involving a piece of technology may therefore affect the future of coaching.

This culminates in a risk that our profession's future may move in a direction that minimises the involvement of human coaches, and doesn't look like professional coaching in its practice.

Notes

1   Manyika, J., Lund, S., Chui, M., Bughin, J., Woetzel, J., Batra, P. et al. (2017) *Jobs lost, jobs gained: What the future of work will mean for jobs, skills, and wages*, McKinsey & Company [report], 28 November. Available at: https://www.mckinsey.com/featured-insights/future-of-work/jobs-lost-jobs-gained-what-the-future-of-work-will-mean-for-jobs-skills-and-wages (accessed 1 October 2020).
2   1 Corinthians 15:2, author's own translation.

13 A bright future (26 minute read)

Rafael spoke to the others, their avatars projected around the table, none of them able to drag their eyes away from the scene unfolding before them.

The AI that had calculated the probability of the missile launch was constantly updating, the percentage hovering around 96% but fluctuating dangerously.

"Anyone finding these social media feeds helpful?" Comfort suddenly barked. She had been in the job three years, and although younger than most world leaders had gained popular support. At the various head shakes and non-committal responses, she swiped the window off the table decisively, drawing the crowd's attention to the AI's suggested actions.

The nuclear response was essentially automated, the only human intervention possible being the Prime Minister providing an override. The instructions had been developed based on Cabinet discussions and an AI tool designed specifically for the task.

Principles for adoption

We've returned throughout this book to the criteria that will determine the areas in the coaching lifecycle most likely to be enhanced by technology. The benefits offered by technology include efficiency, consistency, impact, scope, and sustainability, and we saw several examples of those in Part 2. It's important to bear in mind the trade-off between benefits, costs, risks, and ethics, and it's also important not to be distracted by compelling statistics and emotional statements when our attention should be on making coaching as effective as possible for our coachees. By considering which of the technologies that we've explored offer the greatest benefits with the fewest downsides, we should consciously choose to confidently lean into those key elements of coachtech for which the trade-off makes the most sense.

Remote coaching

It seems sensible to start with the idea of remote coaching, which became the only option for the delivery of coaching for many of us throughout 2020. It will be difficult for anyone to insist on in-person coaching in a post-pandemic world, and so the skills associated with remote delivery, already part of our core competencies, will only become more apparent in the immediate future.

The benefits of remote coaching are broad, and work in the interests of all stakeholders. Without travel time and the risk of upheaval caused by traffic and unexpected events, a typical day can now include more coaching sessions, providing efficiency to us as well as a coaching sponsor. Coupled with the fact that video coaching sessions as a whole tend to be shorter due to our awareness of how draining they can be, it's possible for us to deliver coaching to larger numbers of coachees over more locations than under other circumstances at an attractive price. This further frees up our time to invest in our reflective practice, get things done, or take the chance to regain control over those areas of our lives that have eluded us in the past.

The remote experience also offers a more genuinely consistent approach. In a conversation with a coaching sponsor at one of the big investment banks, I was told of a coaching engagement with a leadership team. Every member of the team had been assigned one of two coaches, both of whom charged the same price per session. When the two invoices arrived at the end of the month, however, one was significantly higher than the other. It turned out that while one coach had been visiting the bank's offices, the other had rented a private room in a nearby club, and had charged this as an additional expense. With remote coaching, every part of the experience with the exception of the coaching itself can be defined by the coachee or the coaching sponsor, giving greater confidence in the consistency of the process and its outputs, and enabling more accurate monitoring of coaching activity over a large population.

The potential additional benefits in the form of collaborative digital workspaces, transcription services, connected technology products, and the like are also appealing options for us, continually enabling us to offer a broader coaching experience with deeper impact. On top of all of this, the thought that delivering coaching remotely will reduce our carbon footprint in many cases paints an unmistakeable picture of the good that remote coaching can offer with the right technology.

All of these positive aspects are available to most of us and our coachees already at no extra cost, so the business case seems plain. Remote coaching is now more than here to stay. It's forming a fundamental foundation of how we will be delivering coaching going forwards, for better or worse. That all said, may we not fall into the trap of conscious ignorance by not paying attention to the risks that remain present as we engage in this most convenient of technologies.

In-session technology enhancements

There is an increasing prevalence of technology in all locations, including in-person coaching conversations, as both we and our coachees are likely to carry smartphones and continuously fancier wearables as the technology develops. This opens up the opportunity for us to use technology within our coaching sessions without disrupting our rapport.

The benefits this brings to our coaching, whether through screen sharing if coaching remotely or through accessing hardware as we meet, like laptops and smartphones, are manifold. We gain an increased capacity for all sorts of creative coaching as we incorporate everything from data analytics to highly visual metaphor powered by VR, and the physical footprint of this varied technology can be minuscule. The days of having to remember a bag full of cards, highlighter pens, and objects to visualise a situational model are now gone, replaced by digital versions that can be permanently present in the form of an app or a website.

Coaching platforms

One of the biggest technology-powered shifts in societal behaviour as a whole has been the creation of peer-to-peer digital marketplaces, like Airbnb and Uber, in the most tangible form of the Connection Economy we have. We will probably all have used one of the offerings out there designed to connect individuals and businesses offering a service to those looking for one. They've grown for a reason, and we should therefore expect the same thing to happen in the coaching space.

Coaching platforms have a lot to offer us as coaches. As a marketing tool, at times they will entirely eliminate the initial stage of trying to find an audience, because the platform's users are already looking for a coach. In conjunction with the administration and management functionality offered, this goes towards saving us a lot of time, not to mention transparency over our coaching engagements and what needs to happen next. The same benefits are on offer for our coachees and coaching sponsors, who now no longer need to rely on word of mouth to source a coach, and can instead find several without leaving their desk chair, and have a granular level of oversight of what's happening with a minimum amount of effort.

The scale made available through these is another enormous benefit. In a frank discussion with a professional executive coach recently, he said that probably ninety-nine out of a hundred sales conversations for him lead to nothing, and so the price he charges has to reflect an investment of his time that's vastly greater than the few hours he will spend coaching. When a coaching platform works, the coachees will come directly to us when they're interested, meaning we can focus our time in a much more targeted manner on the things that will make the biggest difference to us and our coachees. The same is true of a coaching sponsor, who in some cases will only need to interact with one organisation (the platform provider) rather than an endless river of coaches touting for work.

Without forgetting any of the obvious benefits offered by this technology, I can't help but feel drawn back to the associated risks, because of the surge in activity coaching platforms are seeing. The Connection Economy brings baggage. One of a coaching platform's biggest selling points to a coaching sponsor might be that it offers rapid access to coaches at a consistent, low price. And what you feed, grows. In an online marketplace in which we're differentiated more by price and availability than anything else, two things will happen.

Firstly, coachees will find the easiest coaches to book are those who are unable to find work through more traditional routes, meaning some of the best coaches will not get used, and the average quality of coaching will drop as a result. Secondly, the behaviour we will find ourselves driven towards is to reduce our prices purely to remain competitive, which at first glance might be a positive outcome for clients but will have hidden side effects. I know coaches who charge as little as a quarter of their standard coaching rate on coaching platforms so as not to miss out on opportunities; if this continues, it will lead to:

- burnout through us squeezing in more sessions in order to generate an income
- reduced quality of coaching through having to split our time with other work types that provide a steadier income, rather than in improving our coaching practice
- a reduction in empathy for coachees at a systemic level, because the only coaches able to continue operating fully as coaches will be those who don't need to do so due to being in the privileged position of having a passive income, which almost all coachees will not have.

The phrase "the democratisation of coaching" feels like an admirable goal, and yet without quality control and strong relationships, it's no less than a commodification of a valuable service. Given the importance of human interaction in coaching, commodifying us feels like a step in the wrong direction at a time when we need one another more than ever. On top of this fundamental risk, a confidentiality breach of a coaching platform would be devastating. Some of the biggest coaching platforms now have pools of several thousand coaches; if one of their databases was subject to a successful hack, that would be the personal details of thousands upon thousands of individual coachees exposed, and given some of the big corporate clients these platforms are working with, that could include highly sensitive information. It's essentially impossible to protect against a breach of confidentiality with a user base that size, and the potential for the system to become unexpectedly inaccessible is greater than we probably think. While writing this chapter, Amazon Web Services (AWS) suffered an outage affecting its customers, and it has a lot of them – 45% of the world's cloud computing takes place on AWS.[1] If any component in the end-to-end connection between us and a platform failed, all coaching would be prevented from taking place until the incident were to be resolved.

In the early 2010s, several technology issues hit the big banks, leading to ATM outages across the UK for hours and even days at a time. The participants in that value chain that were hit the hardest were those who had built up a reliance on that particular technology – by definition the most vulnerable. Customers who would only ever spend using cash, and businesses who would not accept card, abruptly became unable to do what they had planned to. There's a risk that coaching platforms will become the single point of failure for some coaching value chains, and when that becomes the case, we should be ready with alternative ways of engaging.

Robot coaches

The ability for machines to engage in a productive coaching conversation has already reached a point of possibility. Particularly with performance coaching, focused on behaviour changes that incrementally improve the effectiveness or efficiency of participation in a given process, this narrow application of robot coaching using NLP technology is so close we can taste it. The technology is nowhere near a level at which it could replace all of coaching's activities, and the human presence element sits squarely in the realm of science fiction at present, but the limited deployment described above feels like only a matter of time.

The business case for it is unarguable, because the desired outcome is so clearly defined, and the process is simply a case of automating activities that are currently carried out by us. And as we've seen, machines are far cheaper than we are, have unlimited capacity, and are frustratingly predictable. It is possible to get the same outcome that we could deliver at a fraction of the cost and at a scale that previously would have been unthinkable. It should therefore come as no surprise that the temptation among coaching sponsors will be unanimous to migrate to this sort of solution. In doing so, they will be guaranteeing an identical level of quality across the entire coachee population, offering the ability to analyse data from coaching sessions in a way that has never been achieved before, and exposing more people to the power of coaching while limiting the negative impact on the planet at the same time. How could we fail to support this utopian dream?

As we think about this potential influx of robot coaches to replace us in the performance coaching arena, I've become increasingly aware of our collective tendency towards anthropocentrism. Even when faced with a hypothetical situation in which more coachees will receive better quality outcomes, we rationalise our inclination away from it because of an assumption that humans are superior. And yet the nature of performance coaching is such that machines could categorically do it better than we could; with the right programming, they will always identify boundaries accurately, never fail to concoct the best next question (according to whichever model it's following), and not make the sorts of mistakes we all make. In the early stages of our coach development journey, there's an argument to be made for the benefits of learning to leave our personalities at the door in order to become non-directive and non-judgemental. When we're learning to listen to understand – and ultimately to help our coachee understand – rather than to reply, and conditioning ourselves to use open rather than closed questions, we have to become quite disciplined and even robotic at times in ensuring we remain faithful to a model. Unsurprisingly, that's the sort of thing that machines do far better than we do.

Therefore, providing the risks associated with availability, confidentiality, and so on are mitigated – if possible, eliminated, such as through offline tools that do not retain any conversational data – a seismic shift towards robot coaches is closing in on us fast, and I find it difficult to argue that we shouldn't be in support of it. To counter-balance that, we should be extending our skill-sets right now into arenas that go deeper than performance coaching so that the value we're offering is clearly greater than that on display by the machines.

Client preferences

An overwhelming volume of technology is available for use in coaching, some designed for that purpose and some simply applicable in our activities, giving us the challenge of constantly knowing that there is probably a better way of coaching using technology than we are currently engaging in. This may feel like a new problem but is actually the same sort of thing we've always experienced as coaches, because our coachees are all unique. In fact, one of the elements of coaching I find the most fun is the fact that I truly have no idea how the next session will turn out. In the emergent dance with a coachee, a snapshot of any randomly selected coaching session might see us sitting in silence with our eyes closed, listening to the coachee speak for extended periods, getting close to doing star jumps as an embodied exercise, having quick reflex, high energy brainstorms, exploring metaphors through storytelling, drawing, or poetry, or writing a structure for an organisation's five-year strategic plan.

In the same way, one of the factors that makes every coaching interaction unique will be the coachee's relationship with technology, and given the amount of it out there, the only guarantee is that it will be different from ours. Many decisions around the system-wide use of technology in coaching are going to be entirely out of our hands as individual coaches, and so we have a responsibility to our profession to act ethically in the way we respond to that and to our coachees, to dance to the beat they're hearing with regard to coachtech.

TL;DR

While remembering the importance of the trade-off between the benefits offered by technology and the costs, risks, and ethical dilemmas it presents, we have a duty to wholeheartedly support the introduction of technology that increases the impact of coaching through improving its efficiency, consistency, impact, scope, and sustainability.

Remote coaching provides opportunities for coaching to be delivered to more people at a lower price and in a more convenient way. Our openness to technology in coaching conversations will enhance our flexibility and effectiveness. Similarly, coaching platforms make coaching more accessible, and offer additional benefits to coaching sponsors looking for enhanced insight. Robot coaches, while not truly available yet, will shortly be able to offer performance coaching better than most of us can, and at a significantly reduced cost.

In all uses of coachtech, it is our responsibility to maintain our awareness of our coachees' attitudes and abilities associated with technology so that we might meet them with technology where they are, in order to build rapport, and optimise the effectiveness of our coaching.

Note

1   Greene, J. (2020) Amazon Web Services outage hobbles businesses, *The Washington Post*, 25 November. Available at: https://www.washingtonpost.com/business/economy/amazon-web-services-outage-stymies-businesses/2020/11/25/b54a6106-2f4f-11eb-860d-f7999599cbc2_story.html (accessed 27 November 2020).

14 A likely future (14 minute read)

As the percentage steadily rose and eventually hung at around 98.5%, the high-lighted action moved from "Actively monitor" to "Launch pre-emptive strike". A five-second countdown appeared, and the Prime Minister's avatar glitched, as if terrified into a frozen state. As she winked from view, the countdown finished.

Reappearing, accompanied by a "Bad connection" subtitle, Comfort was greeted by the words "Pre-emptive strike confirmed". Rafael felt his heart plunge deep into his gut.

Comfort's face flashed from perplexity through fury to terror. She looked up at Rafael, her closest ally in the virtual room, her face pleading with him to somehow reverse time or know some way out she didn't.

Surprising himself, Rafael's face suddenly lit up.

"I know what to do!" he exclaimed, and his avatar dimmed, covered by the words ON HOLD.

A few seconds later, he was speaking to someone else.

"Flic" he said, "we don't have time for me to apologise or explain much, but whatever you're in the middle of, this is more urgent." Knowing him the way she did, Flic simply responded with a nod, easily pulling her attention away from an innovative coaching model and fixing it fully on what Rafael was about to say. "I remember you saying you could coach intelligent systems. Could that include convincing a premature automated attack to abort?"

Flic gulped, the enormity of the situation overwhelming her momentarily before being overtaken by her sense of duty. "Send me the details."

Rafael's briefing was succinct and effective, and Flic immediately knew what to do. Her level of concentration almost painful, she connected to the platform that hosted her enhanced cognitive functions, and used her Government clearance to activate the distributed, collective superintelligence feature. As she did so, she drew on the processing power from others with augmentations and at breakneck speed the AI strike system was revisiting its assumptions, recalculating probabilities, and deciding on more effective courses of action.

Precisely which branch of the logic tree the AI dived down to draw its conclusion is unclear, but Flic's eyes remained unfocused as she received her first message of congratulations. She had succeeded in stopping the attack, but at what cost?

What lies ahead

Given everything we've looked at so far, a big question has been closing in on us: What will the future of coachtech actually be like? Are we heading towards a disastrous dystopia, an empowerment-fuelled paradise, or a passive monotony in which the coaching of ten years' time looks essentially the same as the coaching of ten years ago? Of course, it's impossible to predict the future – we have a tendency to overestimate short-term possibilities and underestimate what will happen in the long term. With that in mind, here are some of the key areas I'll be keeping an expectant eye on, and suggest you do the same.

The virtuality continuum

We explored some of the possibilities of VR and AR earlier on. The technology is available now, is actively being developed, and the price for good quality hardware is becoming increasingly justifiable. **Extended reality (XR)**[1] combines the two in an embracing of the full virtuality continuum; the ability to see navigational directions appearing on the road in front of us, and to immediately visit a virtual location within one device.

Unobtrusive XR headsets will become a more popular consumer technology, incorporating productivity and quantified self apps into the vision of their wearers – these have already arrived in some niches such as among keen cyclists, and with adaptable occlusion to prevent light spill, the VR options available will shift the innovation adoption curve forward. Alongside the addition of constantly improving motion capture built into the headset and holoportation, the idea that you and I could meet simultaneously in different locations, speaking different languages, and have essentially no different a sensory experience than we would if we were physically together becomes a reality.[2] We could even spontaneously travel together to exotic locations without either of us leaving our respective homes. While an attractive option on the surface, the ability to escape a reality we can't figure out at whim leads me to wonder whether this is actually a solution, or rather an exacerbation of the problem.

Just as video conferencing moved naturally from an expensive option available only within certain meeting rooms to an almost universally accessible medium, XR devices will become commonplace, albeit over a shorter time period. XR as a meeting tool will become the mode of choice as it becomes more widely accessible, and we'll begin to make significant use of it for remote coaching, as well as for visual and auditory landscapes for reflective exercises, and co-creation of creative content for reflection.

Coaching platforms

We are already starting to see the growth in appetite for coaching platforms that enable potential coachees to access coaching in a streamlined and cost-effective way, and that demand is only going to grow in the short term. We'll begin to feel more explicit pressure to connect to platforms as they continue to move into the organisational coaching space, and begin to offer means by which coaches within one organisation can spend time coaching coachees within another. This will increase as coaching platforms merge and are acquired, perhaps by one of the large ERP (enterprise resource planning) systems.

Over time, coaching platforms will expand to include more explicit support for the coach through live access to coaching models and question banks, enabling even the least experienced of coaches to deliver effective coaching supported by the technology. As more organisations move in the direction of encouraging a coaching culture of leadership, the user base of the platforms will expand to include all people manager roles within organisations, with the line between coaching conversations, performance reviews, and career planning meetings becoming blurred. A belief will emerge within many organisations that peer-to-peer coaching is just as effective as using a qualified coach.

The need for professional coaches will ultimately end up limited to exceptional cases, even when thinking about the most senior levels within an organisation. The role of the professional coach as a result will evolve into a more technically complex one, as the coachees will by their nature bring more difficult contexts and presenting issues. The use of coaching platforms by this point will have become unexceptional, and it will be rare not to use them for professional coaching, even when the coaching itself is happening in an in-person setting, which will remain as an important mode for professional coaching.

Aggregators

With an increase in the use of coaching platforms, specialist coaching tools such as XR apps, licensed coaching question banks, and digital-first coaching models, coachtech providers will shift their primary focus away from the direct user. Rather, they will increasingly position themselves as participants in a longer end-to-end coachtech process, providing access to their application programming interfaces (APIs) rather than directly to the tools themselves, enabling a streamlined coaching experience that draws on relevant expertise.

A new form of coachtech will therefore emerge from the more established technology companies, maybe from one of the big coaching platforms, which aggregates relevant coaching inputs and makes them all accessible within one GUI, rather than having to switch from one piece of technology to another in the middle of a coaching session.

Artificial intelligence

In the coming years, AI will continue to be perceived as lagging behind the quality that we can deliver as human coaches, even as the platforms move more deeply into organisations. As technology continues to advance, and the capabilities of AI for more free-flowing conversation become part of the everyday routine, the big technology companies will begin to offer a therapeutic style of AI coaching to all users as part of a wellbeing agenda through their virtual assistants. Individuals who might otherwise engage in private coaching will begin to default to AI coaches rather than trying to source a human coach.

Despite attempts from the big technology companies to break into the corporate world, the low level of transparency around the cost of internal coaching conversations happening across organisations will prevent a high level of engagement, and a significant volume of performance coaching will continue to be delivered by humans.

After several years, ML trainers will find a way to introduce a more convincing sense of emotion, empathy, and active listening that can replicate much of the coaching experience offered by a human at a functional level. This will have a knock-on effect, leading to a significant reduction in the number of professional coaches. A limited number of coachees will retain a preference for machine-free interaction, protecting the profession from extinction, although its sustainability will rely on more innovative training and accreditation approaches due to the lower number of entrants.

Wearables

A limited level of AI coaching associated with data on the quantified self will grow in popularity, particularly in the wellbeing and relationships arenas. This will emerge as "just in time" coaching notifications, either triggered by certain criteria such as an extended time of elevated heart rate not associated with physical exercise, or heuristic nudges based on behaviour identified as out of the ordinary thanks to its having captured a dataset of expected weekly routines.

As virtual assistant technologies expand into XR technology and brain implants, the coaching AI triggered by wearable data will become indistinguishable from other notifications, encouraging a permanently increased, unconsciously reflective state.

Coaches and technology

The centre of gravity for coachtech capabilities will necessarily have to shift away from performance coaching and towards coaching on a sense of purpose, as a majority of workers whose identities had predominantly been formed by their jobs struggle to adapt to living positively in a world in which they cannot earn an income. The relationship between us as professional coaches and technology – not just coachtech – will have turned a corner in advance of this change of focus, as our roles evolve from users of technology to trainers of it.

The role of the professional coach by this stage, therefore, will be absolutely defined by technology. Far from the coach–coachee relationship being replaced by a robot–coachee relationship, however, it will be replaced by a coach–robot relationship, in which we more than anything else find ourselves coaching the technology itself, enabling in a non-directive manner a state of continuous self-reflection for the technology, so that it will continually learn from its mistakes, return to good practice, and continuously improve.

TL;DR

It's impossible to predict the future, but let's attempt to do just that:

- Many of us will begin to use XR extensively in our coaching, particularly as it becomes part of everyday life.
- Coaching platforms will continue to expand, eventually building in coach support tools until professional coaches are seen as unnecessary in the coaching relationship due to effective peer-to-peer conversations.
- Specialist coachtech products will allow access to interfaces enabling coaching platforms to become a single GUI for multiple technologies.
- AI coaches will emerge from increasingly powerful and intrusive voice assistants from the big technology companies, leading to the coaching profession becoming limited to only a narrow set of high-potential circumstances.
- Wearable technologies will introduce more push notifications, beginning with wellbeing, and expanding into areas traditionally associated with coaching.
- While coachees will default to AI coaches, professional coaches will see the recipients of their coaching becoming the AI that ends up powering portions of society itself.

Notes

1   Also referred to as cross-reality.
2   Foley, M.J. (2019) Microsoft's latest holoportation demo shows off its mixed reality, AI, translation technologies, *ZDNet*, 17 July. Available at: https://www.zdnet.com/article/microsofts-latest-holoportation-demo-shows-off-its-mixed-reality-ai-translation-technologies/ (accessed 11 December 2020).

15 A clarion call to action (15 minute read)

Flic's avatar appeared in Rafael's vision and he angrily accepted the call, feeling his fury rise.

"What happened?" he demanded, his voice taking on a shrill undertone.

"I'm not entirely sure" Flic responded. "The program got to the point of concluding that a pre-emptive strike was the wrong decision, and then cut me off. It looks like it changed direction, though."

"Yes" Rafael replied, his expression stern and his voice quivering with rage, "It seems to have settled on London as a superior target."

Flic's face fell.

Rafael was about to berate her and stopped himself short, made his best attempt at a deep breath, and fixed his gaze on her. "You've signed a death warrant for all of us."

Flic started to respond, confusion, curiosity, and defensiveness each fighting for space, but Rafael interrupted her with a raised finger. His eyes darted around, seeing information Flic wasn't privy to. After a second, his face dropped. "Oh no" he said.

Flic didn't rush him, and a moment later Rafael's focus returned, and he conserved time by simply stating the facts. "Your distributed intelligence network had a security flaw. You didn't convince it to change direction, the Chinese hacked it and diverted it themselves."

What is coaching?

At the outset of this book, we laid out what our definition for coaching is: a conversation-led change tool that is confidential, non-directive, non-judgemental, and challenging. As the technology that supports the delivery and management of coaching continues to develop and expand its use, holding onto that definition is going to become progressively more difficult, not least when the capabilities of technology – and, more practically, its activities – move into the space currently held exclusively by professional coaches.

It's already the case that the boundaries of coaching are rather blurry; some therapy and some coaching could arguably sit in either box, some of the most visible people who call themselves coaches really aren't coaches at all according to this book's definition, and there's very little appetite to attempt to protect the title of "coach" for lots of reasons. For one, coaching principles are being increasingly adopted as desired leadership traits in organisations. What should our philosophy be on coaching if it's seen by some as a protected title held only by an elite group of professionals, whatever definition the word has, and by others as a skillset that should be accessed as circumstances dictate, eliminating the idea of "coaching conversations" altogether?

As that's the context we're sitting in, maybe a movement of technology into coaching isn't as meaningful as it first appears. To put it bluntly: Should we care about the impact of technology on coaching as a practice, or only about its effect on us, the professional coaches?

The coach of the future

Given the potential for technology to expand in its ability and scale, we'll end up with three specific manifestations of coaching, all of which will be relevant regardless of the arena we operate within:

- Non-coaches performing coaching supported by technology
- Technology solutions performing coaching without a human coach present at all
- Professional coaches (whether supported by technology or not).

An assumption we can make is that the expected cost and quality will be greater when using a professional coach than using either of the other approaches. If that's the case, the future role description of a professional coach will need updating to reflect an enhanced level of quality. But what does that mean in practice?

As far as non-coaches are concerned, we already have case studies for this; many managers across organisations will have attended workshops in which they've used a simple coaching model to coach a fellow attendee, at times with some example questions from that model on a sheet in front of them. The natural tendency in these settings is for the conversations to be a pleasant experience for the coachee, highly supportive, with an edge of the person acting as the coach being unable to stop themselves from providing their own opinions and advice.

In contrast, a machine delivering coaching, if programmed to abide by strict coaching protocols, will not provide any advice, and will offer an insightful experience for the coachee, following the model in a more unadulterated manner than a human would. In order to deliver that expected higher level of quality, a professional coach will therefore have to offer what neither the non-coach nor the machine can. The professional coach of the future will have to bring a serrated edge of intuitive, non-directive challenge with an expansive flexibility based on a broad knowledge base, to confidently coach in a potentially ambiguous context.

A need for systemic change

This tighter understanding of professional coaching will require a profession-wide update on competency frameworks and codes of ethics. The current documentation from the professional bodies has developed alongside the evolution of people management in organisations, which are increasingly becoming more coach-like. As technology enables different forms of interaction, there's the potential for the boundaries around our role to be misinterpreted. Perhaps more effort is therefore needed to clarify what about the coaching relationship makes it unique. For example, the ability to use technology well (or at all) doesn't appear as a required coaching competency at present. Given the direction of travel we've discussed in the last few chapters, it will definitely need to in the coming years.

That said, the amount of complexity involved in the world of technology risk, particularly when laid over the intricately creative craft of coaching, is very great. For us to carry that weight of responsibility around with us feels overbearing. To put it bluntly, our brains aren't designed to have to cope with making such big ethical decisions amongst the complexity of the end-to-end chains involved in technology. Our everyday burdens are heavy enough to carry, from recycling to fashion supply chains, all of which seem much more sensible to resolve at the source of the problem, rather than cascading the responsibility to busy, uninformed consumers who could really do with being able to eat a juicy pear without a side order of guilt.

Which brings us back to the professional bodies, who exist for more than mere system-wide definition and generic direction. As coachtech continues to expand its reach, the professional bodies are perfectly positioned to provide support to every stakeholder and not just us as their members. Coachees, coaching sponsors, and technology providers ought to all be engaged in the process of the continuing professionalisation of coaching.

This is already happening in pockets, through thinktanks and coachtech appearing consistently as part of coaching conferences. That said, the centralised voices of the professional bodies have been relatively quiet on the topic, preferring instead to talk in non-specific terms about the volatility of the societal backdrop, and providing CPD sessions that suggest that more is possible while offering very few strong ethical directives. No professional body has recommended or warned against any specific technology, or technology in general, and the most disruptive technology providers are notable by their absence in contexts where the other stakeholders are represented.

As we've seen throughout this book, the complexity at play in the end-to-end coaching experience as far as technology interaction is concerned is too great for us to confidently know that we're making the right decision at every point. As a result, the professional bodies have an opportunity – indeed, a responsibility – to provide clear advice to their members. And the slickest way to do that from the perspective of the ultimate beneficiaries of the coaching is for the professional bodies to offer some sort of credential at the source (for example, the root knowledge base, rules engine, and code of ethics sitting behind a particular AI tool). As much as it should provide comfort to our coachees that we've done our homework and have made the best decision possible with the information available to us, that will never be enough. The chance is too great that we will miss something, be misled by our own biases, or simply not have enough time to do the sort of technical due diligence required to do a proper review of a piece of coachtech. An independent body set up purely to protect the profession, on the other hand, would have the time, skill, and access to provide the right level of comfort to every party involved.

Such a credential would give technology providers permission to move confidently into the coaching arena with the blessing of the profession. It's therefore important that the professional bodies are equipped well enough to pragmatically certify compliant providers, without losing the necessary challenge. Being equipped in this sense means having the right people with access to the right information, which includes a deep understanding of the technology principles as well as a firm conviction about the foundations of coaching. Without that group of genuine experts providing independent assurance over these disruptive influences, we run the risk of good-hearted people who love coaching supporting the adoption of technology that will ultimately unravel that profession, or well-intentioned technology experts with a strong optimism bias recommending products that, while technically excellent, are simply not fit for purpose.

An inspirational future full of potential

The good news is that we have the time to do this, although it's running out quickly. Digital transformation is approaching some industries like a great whale to a shoal of fish, and our profession feels one step away. We have a bit of time to reflect and take a measured response, carefully considering which hills we should die on and which practices we can be more relaxed about losing in light of the benefits to those we are ultimately serving. It's possible to be consciously and appropriately sceptical without tripping into being pessimistic; scepticism is about questioning and validating, and we can do that with an optimistic mindset. Our profession is not doomed, in fact it's becoming increasingly important, and we're so inherently self-aware that we should have confidence that we will respond well to whatever the future throws at us, just as we rose to the challenges of COVID-19.

That all said, perhaps the worst thing any of us can do is to assume that those who will have a hand in leading that response are not each one of us. If you and I each take responsibility for the circles within which we operate, wielding what influence we can, and putting pressure on, and offering support to, those who wield more, surely the entire profession and all of our stakeholders will be stronger as a result. We're collectively building the future of our profession every day through the decisions and actions we take, so should take them consciously with a bright vision in mind. By holding tightly to the fundamentals of what it means to be a coach and embracing the right technology to enhance that capability, we can protect our profession, fulfil our purpose, and benefit those who are relying on us.

Getting things done

That all said, let's get pragmatic. Reflecting on everything we've explored together, we could do worse than take the following steps:

- *Expand our knowledge.* What study could we do to become more understanding of technology?
- *Expect the unexpected.* Even the most basic of technologies encounters issues, so let's have a backup ready to go for every piece of technology we use.
- *Evaluate our landscape.* Create a table containing every piece of technology we use, and the benefits, risks, and ethical dilemmas they present. Then spend time reflecting on what we need to do to optimise our use of it, and which gaps would benefit from expanding our use of technology.
- *Explore with coachees.* Armed with the section headings from Chapter 10, let's ask our coachees what sort of technology they want us to use; coachee readiness is one of the biggest predictors of coaching success, so meeting them with tools they're keen to engage with must be a good place to start.
- *Experiment with something new.* Find a piece of coachtech that intrigues us, and set aside time for unstructured play in it. We want to get comfortable to operate in these new ways. For some of us, it might be an idea to buddy up with another coach, to challenge and stretch one another.
- *Effect systemic change.* Consider whether we could play a role supporting and challenging the professional bodies to provide more direction in the coachtech space.

TL;DR

The expansion of technology into the world of coaching will have an impact on the role of the professional coach. In response to its disruptive influence, we are likely to have to increase the challenge we offer coachees, and continually expand our flexibility across multiple modes of coaching to serve coachees operating in progressively ambiguous contexts.

This will require the professional bodies to update competency frameworks and codes of ethics, at least to include a need for us to understand technology to a certain level. More specifically, the professional bodies have a role to play in providing informed advice to all coaching stakeholders, including in particular technology providers and those investing in coachtech, most likely through the introduction of a specialist coachtech credentialling taskforce.

As coaches ourselves, we should also take responsibility to influence where we can, in the knowledge that the good practice of self-awareness and resilience that fills so much of our world will already act as a partial mitigant to the greatest threats presented by technology.

To get practical, let's take the following steps:

- Expand our knowledge
- Expect the unexpected
- Evaluate our landscape
- Explore with coachees
- Experiment with something new
- Effect systemic change.

Conclusion

The rise of the human coach
(11 minute read)

Every emergency response plan across the UK kicked in almost immediately. With mere minutes left before the certain destruction of London, every ounce of processing power across the country was diverted to solving the most imminent crisis for a generation.

The most advanced AI in existence analysed every action captured by China in fractions of a second, predicting the response to every approach. Threats would be batted away. Begging would be ignored. Reason would be parsed through every propaganda channel in the country and used to justify all-out war.

Only a few seconds after the order was given, the ultimate machine reported back: NO ACTION TAKEN. Rafael didn't have time at that point to probe any further, but had he done so he would have seen the machine stunned into inaction, the outcome least likely to escalate the problem being doing nothing.

"Get me China" he said, and a moment later a communications channel opened up. After a brief greeting, he moved swiftly to the issue at hand. "What can I say that will get you to call off the missile strike?"

His Chinese counterpart looked baffled by the question, and then winked out of sight.

Rafael threw his hands in the air and re-joined the response team, feeling numb. The buzz of activity he was expecting had been concentrated into a focused energy, with every participant hunched over the table. He moved forwards to see, and his breath caught as he saw the path of the missiles now diverted into the mid-Atlantic.

* * *

A fortnight later, and a stream of briefings led the government to conclude that the Chinese hack and missile diversion was fully automated – the Chinese government hadn't even been aware of it. The initial activity that had caused the warning to be raised in the first place turned out to be a Chinese student's poorly written AI script, designed to intercept data at random and write original content based on it. The data it captured was the UK government's coaching platform.

Rafael settled back into his chair, having replayed his actions from different angles, carefully discovering things about himself and deciding on actions to tighten up the systems, before standing with an energy that said: I'm grateful for today. Flic stood up too, and they shook hands, warmly.

"See you next month" Flic said with a smile, escorting him to the door and closing it delicately behind him.

Rafael descended the steps, noticing the sounds of his feet on the clean concrete and the chirps of birds drifting in from Hyde Park, and decided he would walk to his next meeting.

The difficulty with writing this book has been in presenting the facts in an interesting way, while remaining aware that the emotions it has been evoking in me could cloud the issues if I weren't careful. I'm curious to know what you felt as thoughts bubbled up of what's possible, how technology could transform the face of coaching, and what might go wrong. The emotions that emerged for me as I explored these concepts included excitement at the capabilities of technology, a deep sense of satisfaction in my coaching being enhanced, disappointment at my own habits, and at times outright terror for our future. And with all of those emotions as a backdrop, I'm keen to lead us all to ask what actions we ought to take; what will you do differently as a result of reading this book?

I can't know what your current relationship with technology is like and how it impacts on your coaching practice. Regardless of how mature you'd describe your relationship with coachtech, we all ought to respond to what we're learning with considered action. We should ensure that we optimise our use of technology to maximise the benefits for the whole coaching profession ecosystem, while maintaining our awareness of the risks and the ethical dilemmas. That means:

- developing a toolkit of coachtech products just as we have developed a toolkit of coaching models and exercises
- paying attention to our coachees' needs, and calling on the right technologies at the right times to meet them
- building a clear framework that makes decision-making around technology that we have questions over much more straightforward, such as a rule that we will never risk any coaching conversation content falling into the wrong hands.

If we do this, our entire profession will be protected from the system-wide risks we are all collectively subject to, whether directly or indirectly. In the words of Martin Luther King, "We are caught in an inescapable network of mutuality, tied in a single garment of destiny. Whatever affects one directly, affects all indirectly."[1] At present, the majority of coaching in the world is still done by people, and it isn't obvious how long that's going to continue to be the case. If we stand up for the principles we've discussed in this book, and influence those around us to do the same, then when the next earth-shattering event takes place to pull the rug out from under our profession, we will have already laid the foundations for a resilient and sustainable response.

At times, this might need us to take the courageous step of speaking out in an informed way against technologies that undermine the important cornerstones of coaching. When a person or an organisation we're connected to installs a new coaching app featuring the ability to provide tailored advice, we should be calling it out as something other than coaching.

At others, we might feel called upon to engage directly with the professional bodies to offer support as they move forward with their ethical responsibilities. Perhaps our united actions as coaches across the profession will mean that there is no need for them to expand into certifying the appropriateness of technology platforms, or perhaps one of the members of the first group to do just that is reading these words right at this instant.

To summarise this entire book in one abstract idea, we are called to shift our mindset away from a technology-led, short-term, attention-hijacked, efficiency-obsessed view of coaching, and forcefully towards a more eternally present and transcendent coaching consciousness that sees our use of technology from the perspective of our clients' grandchildren more than from their shareholders. If we do that, and influence technology providers to do the same, maybe humanity as a whole will thank us.

I'm genuinely energised about where the coaching profession will go next. The time of fad coaches jumping into the scene to make a quick return without the best interests of their clients at heart is coming to an end, and we're well positioned – thanks in large part to technology – to unashamedly bang the drum loudly for what coaching truly stands for. The roots of coaching actually lie in what makes us human at our core, and as the professional bodies continue their own journeys, I believe we're on the cusp of a new wave of professionalisation aligned to that vision.

There will always be some things that technology will be able to do better than us, and as a general rule they are the things that we don't really enjoy doing. The things we can do to differentiate ourselves from the machines, therefore, are to stop acting like robots, and start giving coachees that which only we are able to give: ourselves. The thing that makes coaching work at all, and the thing that makes exceptionally brilliant coaches able to deliver those stand-out results, is in our ability to be the truest version of a human with our coachees, and for our coaching to have that impact too.

One of the foundational pillars of my childhood was watching Laurel and Hardy, and almost every comedy duo since has labelled them as inspirations and masters of their craft. What's interesting about them is that despite being well-connected, skilled, and experienced writers and performers in their own right, their solo careers remain a footnote. After Ollie Hardy died, Stan Laurel continued to write material for Laurel and Hardy, and declined every offer to partner with other actors; it turns out that their magic came from the human connection they shared.

In a similar way, our gift to the world can be in the human connection we build with our coachees. Technology can provide miraculous ways to achieve just that – how else could we tangibly share moments of deep connection with someone on the other side of the world without technology? Let's double down on our commitment to being the best coaches we can be, bringing a deeper sort of magic to the world than any machine ever will.

Note

1   King, M.L. (1963) "Letter from a Birmingham Jail [King, Jr.]", African Studies Center, University of Pennsylvania. Available at: https://www.africa.upenn.edu/Articles_Gen/Letter_Birmingham.html (accessed 7 October 2020).

Glossary

Application programming interface (API): Standardised code providing connectivity to an application that can be accessed by developers in a consistent manner

Artificial intelligence (AI): Computer systems that perform tasks traditionally requiring human intelligence

Augmented reality (AR): The addition of digital imagery onto a live camera feed

Big data: Unimaginably large datasets containing a diverse range of data, often being continually updated and analysed in real-time

Customer relationship management (CRM) system: a data repository containing all relevant information about customers and prospects

Dark web: The portion of the internet not indexed by search engines, requiring anonymisation and authorisation to access

Encryption: applying a process to data that makes it unreadable to those without the right encryption key. In increasing security, encryption can be:

- symmetric, in which the data is encrypted and decrypted with the same key
- asymmetric, in which data is encrypted with a public key for a specified recipient, who can unlock it with the corresponding private key known only to them
- zero-knowledge (also known as end-to-end), in which a key pair is generated in such a manner that the encryption provider does not have access to it

Extended reality (XR): A platform allowing access to both VR and AR technology

Internet of Things (IoT): The network of physical objects containing functionality that connects to the internet

Machine learning (ML): Computer systems that learn and adapt using a rules engine and predictive analysis rather than following traditional, linear programming techniques

Natural language processing (NLP): machines designed to respond to commands given in the user's natural language

Virtual reality (VR): Technology that detects the user's movement to immerse them in virtual locations

Bibliography

Bostrom, N. (2014) *Superintelligence*, Oxford: Oxford University Press.

Boyce, A.L. and Clutterbuck, D. (2011) E-coaching: Accept it, it's here, and it's evolving!, in G. Hernez-Broome and L.A. Boyce (eds.) *Advancing Executive Coaching: Setting the Course for Successful Leadership Coaching*, San Francisco, CA: Jossey-Bass.

Christian, B. and Griffiths, T.L. (2016) *Algorithms to Live By: The Computer Science of Human Decisions*, New York: Henry Holt.

Deniers, C. (2019) Experiences of receiving career coaching via Skype: An interpretative phenomenological analysis, *International Journal of Evidence Based Coaching and Mentoring*, 17 (1): 72–81. Available at: https://radar.brookes.ac.uk/radar/items/f1718293-f3d1-4cfa-9166-dc72958887a3/1/.

Kanatouri, S. (2020) *The Digital Coach*, Abingdon: Routledge.

McLaughlin, M. (2013) Less is more: The executive coach's experience of working on the telephone, *International Journal of Evidence Based Coaching and Mentoring*, S7: 1–13. Available at: https://radar.brookes.ac.uk/radar/items/496377b3-7e90-4288-851e-f4d9a62fe79a/1/.

Mori, M. (1970) The uncanny valley, *Energy*, 7 (4): 33–35.

Open Data Institute (2019) *Data Ethics Canvas*. Available at: https://theodi.org/wp-content/uploads/2019/07/ODI-Data-Ethics-Canvas-2019-05.pdf (accessed 5 October 2020)

Pascal, A., Sass, M. and Gregory, J.B. (2015) I'm only human: The role of technology in coaching, *Consulting Psychology Journal: Practice and Research*, 67 (2): 100–109.

Perez, C.C. (2019) *Invisible Women: Exposing Data Bias in a World Designed for Men*, London: Chatto & Windus.

Ribbers, A. (2015) *E-Coaching: Theory and Practice for a New Online Approach to Coaching*, Abingdon: Routledge.

Suler, J. (2015) *Psychology of the Digital Age: Humans Become Electric*, Cambridge: Cambridge University Press.

Terblanche, N. (2020) A design framework to create Artificial Intelligence Coaches, *International Journal of Evidence Based Coaching and Mentoring*, 18 (2): 152–165. Available at: https://radar.brookes.ac.uk/radar/items/312d40ec-ccdf-431c-a062-2aa862166ac4/1/.

Tompkins, P. and Lawley, J. (2000) *Metaphors in Mind: Transformation Through Symbolic Modelling*, London: Developing Company Press.

Wang, A., Singh, A., Michael, J., Hill, F., Levy, O. and Bowman, S.R. (2019) GLUE: A multi-task benchmark and analysis platform for natural language understanding, Paper presented at the *7th International Conference on Learning Representations, ICLR 2019*, New Orleans, LA, 6–9 May. Available at: https://openreview.net/pdf?id=rJ4k-m2R5t7 (accessed 23 September 2020).

Wernham, L. (2011) *The social media coach: Social media and coaching. A qualitative study of coach practice*, Available at: https://2coach.files.wordpress.com/2012/03/social_media_coaching_research_lynnwernham1.pdf (accessed 18 November 2020).

Yaden, D.B., Eichstaedt, J.C. and Medaglia, J.D. (2018) The future of technology in positive psychology: Methodological advances in the science of well-being, *Frontiers in Psychology*, 9: 962. Available at: https://doi.org/10.3389/fpsyg.2018.00962.

Index